EGYPTIAN
MYTHOLOGY

EGYPTIAN
MYTHOLOGY

SIMON GOODENOUGH

TIGER BOOKS INTERNATIONAL
LONDON

This edition published in 1997 by
Tiger Books International PLC, Twickenham

This book was designed and produced by
Todtri Productions Limited P.O. Box 572, New York,
NY 10116-0572 FAX: (212) 695-6988

Printed and bound in Singapore

ISBN 1-85501-933-7

Author: Simon Goodenough

Publisher: Robert M. Tod
Designer: Vic Giolitto
Art Director: Ron Pickless
Editor: Nicolas Wright
Typeset and DTP: Blanc Verso/UK

Contents

Introduction

At first glance, the ancient Egyptians and their gods appear formal and distant from everyday life as we know it. Everything they had was intended to impress, and so it does. The remains of vast temples, massive pyramids, rows of carvings in relief, stylized images, and rigid postures, along with their amazing paraphernalia of wealth, is evidence of ancient Egyptian pomp and power. The extensive numbers of gods and goddesses, the complex combinations of their names, the overlapping of their roles, and the multiplicity of local variations on their myths can be confusing. For a people perceived as so ordered, so conscientious in recording whatever happened to them, their gods seem to lack any order at all. The overwhelming physical remains of their civilization coupled with this awkward divinity, scarcely seem relevant to the lives of ordinary people today.

Look further and you may marvel at the little details of life that have survived. Look at the pictures on the walls of an Egyptian tomb and you will find pictures of families living in great domesticity: Children holding on to their parents and playing; fishermen and bird catchers casting their nets; farmers working in the field—plough-

Above: The ordinary people of Egypt worshiped their gods in many different ways, often engaging in exuberant dancing to celebrate a successful harvest or other such event.

ing, sowing, reaping, and irrigating the land with precious water from the River Nile; traders bringing home luxuries from abroad to fashion-conscious men and women; and beautifully observed and delicately drawn creatures and plants of all kinds.

Look more closely at the details of the gods and goddesses. The strange shapes of their heads and bodies (when they are not in human form) are of birds and animals familiar to the ordinary Egyptian living along the Nile and in its delta region. There are crocodiles and hippopotami; lions, apes, cows, bulls, rams, wolves, jackals, cats, dogs, scorpions, scarabs, and snakes; and vultures, ibis, and assorted birds of prey. All creatures of significance had their parallel among the gods, and all human activity had its divine guardians and protectors.

There were gods representing all of the dominant features of life such as the River Nile, the air, the sky, and the earth. There were also gods of childbirth and medicine, protectors against injury, gods of learning and of scribes, of a woman's toilet and of marriage, and of architecture, music, art, and science. At the end of person's life, there were gods of death to take them by the hand, judge them for how they had behaved in life, and reward them with eternal pleasures in the next world or let divine scavengers devour them.

It was important, therefore, that people were able to recognize the appropriate god for each occasion. Objects worn or carried by the gods were a form of shorthand that symbolized their responsibilities in the real world. Every Egyptian knew what these objects meant and would welcome any god's protection. In a way, the gods were everyday companions of the ordinary people, and this was reinforced by everyday weaknesses that many gods revealed in the myths. They too became old and senile, might become drunk, or have violent and disruptive passions. They argued, played tricks, and revenged themselves on one another—even as they exerted the magical and ritual powers that people expected of them.

The world of the gods mirrored that of humans in every way. The gods reflected and influenced the political structure of the country. Initially, even the most renown national gods, such as Ra and Osiris, were only important in specific towns. In different regions, several gods might have similar responsibilities. As towns like Memphis and Thebes grew in importance, and as their kings established dynasties that ruled Egypt in its entirety, the influence of their local gods spread and less influential gods of similar aspect merged with them to combine or share their names and duties.

It was politically expedient for the king to promote the power of his own local god to gain reflected glory. It was also in the interests of the temple priests to acquire greater influence and wealth. Acceptance and worship of influential gods was a key tool in unifying the state of Egypt. To cement alliances, advantageous marriages were arranged among the rulers on earth, just as they were arranged among the gods in myth. The sense of awe among the people at the magnificence of the temples was another tool that the king used effectively by linking his own fortunes to those of a god. The pharaoh represented a god himself, and his human authority was thus reinforced.

All of the above made sense in a land that could easily break up into dislocated and vulnerable regions. It was a system that worked to the advantage of the people themselves. A stable state and a strong pharaoh who could mediate on the people's behalf with the gods were vital considerations to ensure a comfortable life and to build up hopes for the afterlife. Egyptians enjoyed life and were obsessed by death. They believed firmly in life after death but they wished to leave nothing to chance. They ordered their existence and their gods as a form of insurance that was both a magnificent display of confidence and the evidence of human frailty.

Below: Images of the goddess Ma'at flank cartouches of Set I with their protective wings.

THE WORLD OF
EGYPTIAN MYTHOLOGY

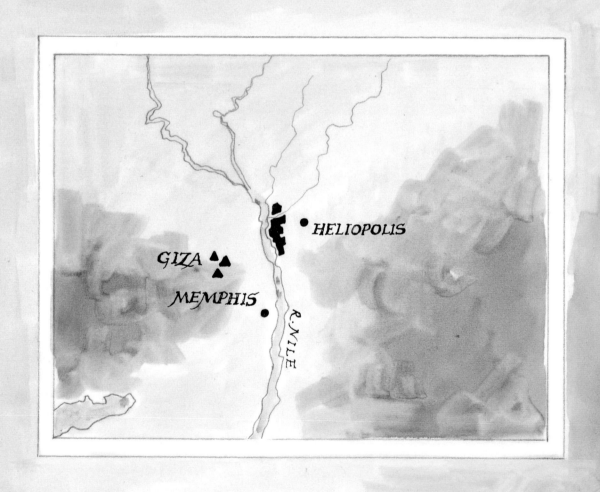

Chapter One
A Rich History

ncient Egyptian civilization was concentrated on a narrow strip of fertile territory along the River Nile with deserts on both sides. At its northern end, Egypt spreads out into the wide, flat space of the Nile delta. At the point where it begins to broaden out, there was a fertile plain known as the Faiyum, on which the Egyptians greatly depended for food. The Mediterranean Sea, which the Egyptians called the Uat-ur or Wadj-ur (the Great Green), formed the country's northern border. Until the time of the Middle Kingdom, the southern border was considered the First Cataract at Aswan. However, there had been previous excursions beyond that point. The border was extended 250 miles (402 km) south during the Middle Kingdom, and about 600 miles (965 km) south during the New Kingdom. The eastern boundary was the Red Sea and to the west was the Libyan desert.

Opposite: The ancient Egyptians never saw the Sphinx floodlit at night; nevertheless, the inspiring scene is well suited to their own sense of drama.

Below: The ankh (a cross with a loop at the top) was the symbol of eternal life in ancient Egypt, shown here in the detail of a relief from the Philae Temple at Aswan.

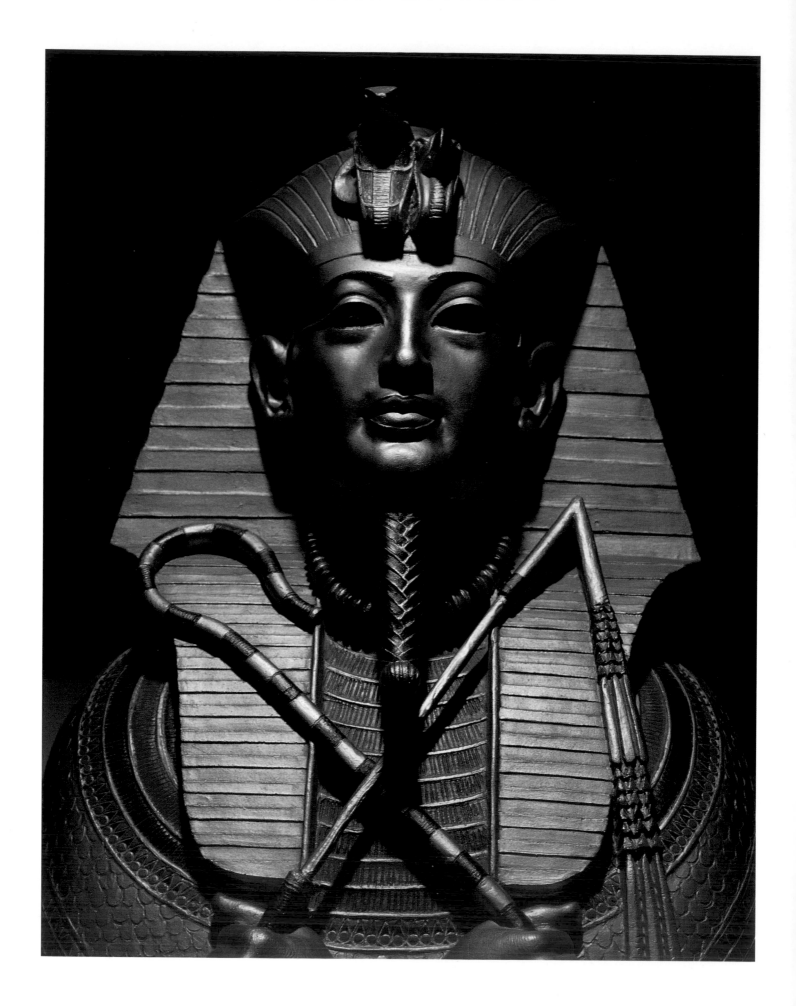

Geographical Divisions

Traditionally, Egypt was divided into Upper Egypt in the south (which extended north to Assiut), and Lower Egypt in the north. Three thousand years before Christ, these areas were considered two separate kingdoms. Not much is known about the formal structure of their organization because there is little evidence still in existence today. Upper Egypt, known as Ta-resu, had its capital at Nekheb (now represented by the ruins of Al Kab). This area was presided over by the goddess Nekhbet, whose symbol was a vulture. Lower Egypt, known as Ta-Meht, had its ancient capital at Buto in the delta and was presided over by a goddess of the same name, whose symbol was a cobra.

The nature of the land in the north and south was very different. The widespread fertile lands of the northern delta—which once had seven rivers flowing through it—were enriched by layers of effluvium and silt from the annual inundation of the Nile. The main features of the south were the sandstone cliffs along the Nile and the massive outcrops of granite that sometimes came right up to the river, and at times left space for areas of fertilization along the banks.

With its natural geographical barriers, Egypt focused its early stages on the Nile itself, which drew north and south together in a remarkable cooperation. Early settlers formed various sites in both Upper and Lower Egypt.

This period was known as pre-dynastic, which was before the formal history of Egypt began. The formal history was initiated with the unification of

Opposite: Golden mask of Tutankhamun. Facsimile from the Egyptian Museum, San José, California. The richness of the discoveries in the tomb of the boy-king have made him one of the most famous of all pharaohs.

Left: Granite statue of the Pharaoh Amenhotep IV, later known as Akhenaten, who renounced worship of Amon and promoted the cult of the god Aten. His obsession with religion weakened Egypt's power.

Following pages: The Temple of Ramesses II at Abu Simbel. The most striking feature of this famous shrine, dedicated to the god Amon and to Ramesses himself, are the four colossal statues of the pharaoh.

Above: The Temple of Luxor, at Thebes, was dedicated to the god Amon, erected by the pharaoh Amenhotep III, and added to by Ramesses II. The great temples of ancient Egypt all grew over a time period lasting several reigns.

northern and southern Egypt by King Menes in about 3100 B.C. This unification was a vital moment in the development of the country. Menes founded his capital at Memphis near present-day Cairo, and it remained the capital of Egypt for about 1000 years.

A Long Political History

The Egyptian historian and priest Manetho, who wrote in Greek in the middle of the third century B.C., divided the rulers of Egypt into thirty dynasties (or families) starting with King Menes. Later, historians grouped these dynasties into the Old, Middle, and New Kingdoms, which coincided with the three main periods of Egypt's greatness. In between these kingdoms, there were intermediate periods where there was instability and chaos because more than one dynasty was ruling in more than one area of Egypt at the same time. Within this framework and with fluctuating fortunes, the distinctive character of Egyptian civilization remained little changed for 3000 years. Then in 30 B.C., Egypt became part of the Roman Empire.

The words king and pharaoh are largely interchangeable. Pharaoh was a title for the king, though originally it meant the great house in which the king lived.

The Early Dynastic Period

There are disagreements among historians about the precise dates of the early
periods in Egyptian history, but they do not differ that much. What is known as
the early dynastic period, starting with King Menes and the first dynasty, ran
from about 3000 B.C. to about 2600 B.C., which was near the end of the third
dynasty. No one is certain whether the kings of the first and second dynasties were
buried at Saqqarah near Memphis, or farther up the Nile at Abydos. The tombs at
both places have been robbed and burned, so that identification is impossible.
In both cases, the tombs were made of mastabas, which were unbaked mud brick
set over pits cut into the rock. The burial chamber was surrounded by rooms containing offerings of wine, beer, oil, or sometimes entire meals. It was filled
with furniture, stone, and pottery vases, along with copper tools and hunting
weapons for use in the next world. The Egyptians already had a strong belief

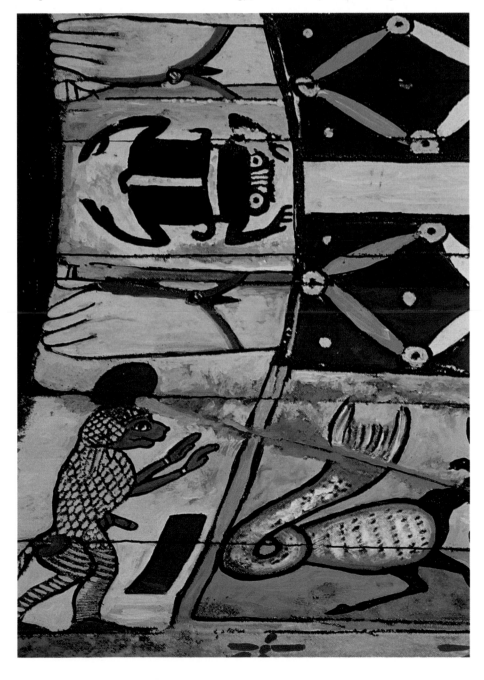

*Left: The scarab beetle, painted between the feet of the
deceased on a coffin lid from Egypt. The mummy is circa
second century A.D. The Egyptians wore amulets in the form
of the beetle, which was associated with the life-giving sun.*

Right: The Alabaster Sphinx of Memphis, the capital city of ancient Egypt from the Early Dynastic period. The Sphinx emerged during the fourth dynasty as a symbol of royal power.

in the afterlife and a high degree of skill as artesans and craftsmen.

The cohesion of Upper and Lower Egypt probably took some time and was not complete until the end of the second dynasty, when the first period of Egypt's greatness really began. The great step pyramid at Saqqarah was built in the third dynasty by the architect and learned scribe Imhotep for the king Zoser (or Djoser). The pyramid was surrounded by a complex of marvelous, white limestone temples for the funerary cult. Imhotep was skilled as doctor and famed as a magician. Later, he himself was regarded as a god.

The Old Kingdom

The Old Kingdom was the first period of real greatness for Egypt. It ran from the fourth to sixth dynasties, around 2600 B.C. to about 2100 B.C. The fourth dynasty produced the most renowned remains in Egypt: the three great pyramids of Giza built by Cheops (known also as Khufu), Chephren (or Khafra), and Mycerinus (or

Opposite: Hatsheput's Temple at western Thebes. Queen Hatsheput ruled Egypt successfully for fifteen years, assuming all the responsibilities of a pharaoh.

*Above: An Egyptian pharaoh worshiping in the temple.
Pharaohs had a priest-king role and were regarded as inter-
mediaries between the people and the gods.*

*Previous pages: Thebes was one of the most important capital
cities in ancient Egypt. These are the Colossi of Memnon, in
quartzite sandstone, on the west bank of the Nile at Thebes;
they represent the pharaoh Amenhotep III. The northern statue, on the right, is known as the shrieking statue.*

Menkare); and the Sphinx, which stands next to the pyramid of Chephren. These
pyramids were considered by the Greeks to be one of the Seven Wonders of the
World. Each was surrounded by smaller pyramids and mastabas for members of
the royal family, and a funerary temple.

The period from the fourth to the sixth dynasties was the age of the great pyramid builders. It was also a period of growing confidence. When the fourth-dynasty
king Sneferu successfully raided Nubia and Libya, he received forty vessels laden
with timber from the forests of Lebanon and arts and crafts flourished. In the fifth
dynasty (because of the influence of the priests of Heliopolis), worship of the god
Ra or Re (the sun god of Heliopolis), supplanted worship of the god Horus. There
was an increasing number of foreign expeditions to Sinai, Libya, and further south.
The longest reigning king in Egyptian history was Pepi II, who ruled for ninety-
four years. However, his great age and eventual senility led to the undermining of
his authority. Central power was weakened and the provinces (or nomes) led by
their monarchs became increasingly independent.

The seventh and eighth dynasties lost control of their territories, and the capital
of the ninth and tenth dynasties moved from Memphis further south to
Herakleopolis in the Faiyum. During this time, Asians and Libyans encroached on
the delta region. The dynasties at Herakleopolis, in turn, lost control to the southern nomarchs of Thebes led by the general Mentuhotpe II. He established the
eleventh dynasty and a new, strong central government that reunited Egypt during
the years of the Middle Kingdom.

The Middle Kingdom

This was the second period of Egypt's strength, running from the eleventh to fourteenth dynasties—from about 2000 B.C. to about 1640 B.C.—when the central state began to break up again. The eleventh dynasty started a military push into Nubia, Libya, the Sinai, and Palestine. That dynasty, in turn, was displaced by a military commander named Amenemhet who stamped his authority on the land by sailing up and down the Nile with a strong fleet. He also built a new capital at Ith-tawy (Lisht), south of Memphis.

During this period, defensive walls were built on the eastern frontier and expeditions were sent to the Red Sea and further south—as far as the Third Cataract of the Nile. Nubia was brought under Egyptian control and its mines contributed to the growing wealth of Egypt. The land in the Faiyum was reclaimed for agriculture. Huge pyramids were built at Ith-tawy and Dahshur, and a complex mortuary temple known as the Labrynth was constructed. An Egyptian named Nefrusobek became the first woman to assume all the titles of a pharaoh, but she only ruled for four years.

Below: Burial chamber of the young pharaoh Tutankhamun. He was probably only eight or nine years old when he succeeded to the throne, and died of a head wound before he was twenty.

Once again during the thirteenth and fourteenth dynasties, Egypt broke up into disunited areas, partly influenced by the growing number of Asian peoples who had infiltrated into the delta. Of these Asians, the Hyksos began to dominate the land during the fifteenth and sixteenth dynasties. They ruled simultaneously with the purely Egyptian seventeenth dynasty. The Egyptians (based at Thebes in Upper Egypt) began to fight the Hyksos. During the eighteenth dynasty, founded by Ahmose I, the Hyksos were finally ousted from Egypt altogether. He introduced the New Kingdom, which was historically Egypt's most prestigious period.

Above: Queen Nefertiti, wife of the pharaoh Akhenaten, was considered one of the most beautiful women in Egypt. She shared her husband's religious enthusiasm and here is seen performing a ceremony.

The New Kingdom

Sometimes known as the New Empire, this period ran from the eighteenth to the twentieth dynasties, from about 1550 B.C. to about 1070 B.C. Under Ahmose I, Amon (the god of Thebes) became the state god of Egypt, and the temples of Karnak and Luxor were expanded. Ahmose established a strong central government and the Viceroyalty of Nubia.

Under Thutmose I, the third king of that dynasty, Egypt conquered territories as far as the Euphrates. Thutmose was the first of many kings to be buried in the Valley of the Tombs of the Kings at Thebes. His grandson Thutmose III was one of the most successful military commanders in Egyptian history. During the childhood of Thutmose III, Egypt was ruled by Queen Hatsheput (a regent), who made considerable contributions to Egypt's success. She encouraged the arts and architecture, sent expeditions to the land of Punt (south of the Red Sea), while managing to maintain peace at home. She finally abdicated and was possibly killed at the instigation of Thutmose to make sure she was out of his way.

Thutmose waged several successful military campaigns, acquired immense amounts of booty, and established a highly efficient administration. His son Amenhotep II was a great athlete and sportsman. His great grandson Amenhotep III was an enthusiastic

Opposite: The coffin for the mummy of Ramesses II. He went on his first campaign with his father when he was only fourteen, and lived to the age of ninety-six. He built some of the greatest structures of ancient Egypt.

Right: Cleopatra was the last ruler of Egypt before control passed to the Romans.

Previous pages: The pyramids dominate the region, with minor grave complexes and religious sites in the foreground. After the pyramids were built, nonroyal officials also insisted on being buried near the site.

builder, adding hugely to the temples of Karnak and Luxor. He constructed his own vast funerary temple and a great lake for his wife, Queen Tiy. All this was paid for by the immense wealth pouring into Egypt from its conquered territories.

Amenhotep IV was a remarkable person and a religious fanatic who abandoned the traditional and established worship of Amon, and the capital at Thebes with its powerful and wealthy priests. He imposed on the whole country the cult of Aten— a form of the sun god Ra—as the visible source of creation and vitality. Amenhotep IV was married to Queen Nefertiti, who was reputed to be one of the most beautiful and fascinating women in ancient Egypt. When he built a new capital at Amarna, he erased the name of Amon from every possible monument. He himself changed his own name from Amenhotep ("Amon is satisfied") to Akhenaten ("it pleases Aten"). He concentrated so heavily on this obsession that he ignored the governance of Egypt and the threats on its borders. Therein followed a short period of severe decline in Egypt's fortunes.

His immediate successors ruled briefly. The second was the boy pharaoh Tutankhamun, who reverted the state back to the worship of Amon. He also changed his own name from its original, Tutankhaten. His tomb produced some of the best remains of ancient Egypt, which have been displayed around the world. Subsequently, it was the general Horemhab who re-established Egypt's strength and reaffirmed the state worship of Amon. The ordinary people had probably never abandoned him in any case.

Another famous name, that of Ramesses, followed Horemhab. Ramesses I began

30

ruling in the nineteenth dynasty. However, it was his grandson Ramesses II (known as the Ramesses the great), who once more established Egypt's power during a reign of more than sixty years. He won victories against Egypt's enemies (the Nubians, Libyans, Syrians, and Hittites), completed the great hall of pillars at Karnak begun by his grandfather, built magnificent monuments to his victories, was responsible for the rock temple at Abu Simbel, and the mortuary temple known as the Ramessum.

As Ramesses II grew old, weakened, and died, the Libyans and the "people from the sea" once again threatened Egypt. There was a brief return to glory in the twentieth dynasty during the reign of Ramesses III. He built a magnificent temple adorned with scenes of his victories at his palace on the edge of Thebes, and managed to avoid an assassination plot which was initiated by his harem. Several pharaohs named Ramesses succeeded him, but during their reigns Egypt fell into decline again and many of their tombs were robbed or destroyed. During the reign of the last one, the priests of Amon usurped the title of pharaoh even before the king was dead.

While the priests ruled Upper Egypt from Thebes, another dynasty—the kings of Tanis—ruled the delta lands. At the same time, the Libyans also held Egyptian territory based at Bubastis in the delta. They gained some control over Thebes, but an independent line of kings set up divided rule. Records of these dynasties are scarce. There were a number of kings ruling over different areas. A separate kingdom was established in Cush with its capital at Napata near the Fourth Cataract. Egypt was then subject to strong a Nubian influence until the Assyrians moved in. They conquered Egypt and installed a governor. When the Assyrians were expelled a Babylonian threat was repelled, but Egypt succumbed to the Persians who intermittently dominated the country through a succession of dynasties between 525 and 335 B.C.

In 332 B.C., Alexander the great won control of Egypt, founded the city of Alexandria, and was succeeded by his general Ptolemy. Greek rule continued until Cleopatra came to power and the general Octavius (later to become the Emperor Augustus) established Roman control and Egypt lost its independence for good.

Below: The Sphinx and pyramids at Giza, the plateau southwest of modern Cairo where the Old Kingdom royal families built their necropolis.

Chapter Two
Creation, Birth & Death

Like most civilizations, the ancient Egyptians created a rich tapestry of myths, gods, and goddesses to explain mysteries such as life, death, and the creation of the world. Their beliefs were deeply ingrained in their everyday lives as the surviving ruins of their temples and tombs can attest.

The Creation Myths

The main Egyptian myths of creation originate from four different parts of the country. They are not wholly distinct because in time they borrowed from each other and overlapped. There were undoubtedly many other local variations that disappeared beneath the dominance of these myths.

Opposite: Granite statue of Akhenaten, who believed that the priests of the god Amon were becoming too powerful, and so replaced the god with Aten. Spiritual issues were closely linked to political ends.

Below: Detail from a painting on a mummy case showing a deceased Egyptian being carried on the back of the sacred bull. Egyptians believed fervently in life after death, and in the rituals and myths associated with death.

Above: The solar boat, with seven of the eight gods, the sacred beetle, and the solar disk, making their way across the heavens. From the Papyrus of Anhai.

Opposite: Facsimile of an original bust of the beautiful Nefertiti, wife of Akhenaten, in the Berlin Museum. In the minds of the people, pharaohs and their consorts were closely associated with the gods.

Heliopolis

There is little information about this set of myths arising from the Old Kingdom, probably because the stories were so well known in their time that people assumed they did not need to be written down.

According to the people of Heliopolis, the world began with the water of chaos (known as Nun), from whom emerged Atum. Atum bore within him the sum of all existence. At first, Atum was only a local god of Heliopolis. However, once he was identified with the god Ra, Atum became more significant. He was personified as the setting sun and the sun before its rising.

Having appeared on a hill where later his temple stood, Atum created other gods and goddesses by masturbation. His son Shu (god of air) and Shu's twin sister Tefnut (goddess of moisture) were born by being spat or vomited out of Atum's

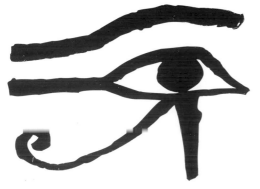

mouth. Shu and Tefnut gave birth to Nut (the sky goddess, whom Shu is often shown holding aloft) and Geb (the earth god, lying at Shu's feet). Nut and Geb gave birth to Isis, Osiris, Nephthys, and Set. These nine, including Atum, were known as the Ennead of Heliopolis. They, together with the other gods and goddesses associated with them, gave rise to a whole range of myths.

Hermopolis

The creation myth of Hermopolis was similar in some ways to that of Heliopolis, but it focused on eight original gods known as the Ogdoad. Nun (the frog-headed

Right: The Temple of Hather, at Dendera, houses the oldest circular zodiac of ancient times. The Egyptians observed the stars but did not speculate on their properties.

Previous pages, left: Worship of the goddess Isis, one of the most beloved goddesses of ancient Egypt. She was particularly popular during Greek and Roman times.

Previous pages, left, below: The Eye of Horus, known as the wadjet, or "healthy eye," one of the most potent symbols of ancient Egypt, representing the eye lost by the god Horus in the fight to avenge the death of his father, Osiris. The Eye was restored by Isis.

Previous pages, right: The massive statue of the head of the Pharaoh Ramesses II, at the entrance to the Temple of Luxor. There was no doubt that the pharaohs expected their names and reputations to last forever.

god) still represented the waters of chaos together with his consort Naunet who had a serpent's head. There were also the married couples Huh and Hauhet (endlessness or eternity), Kuk and Kauket (darkness), and Amon and Amaunet (air or invisibility). Amon (the hidden one) became the most important of these. He stirred up the waters and the darkness to bring about life, ensuring the rising of the sun and inundation of the Nile. Associated with this myth was the concept of a cosmic egg laid by a celestial goose or an ibis.

Memphis

According to the priests of Memphis, it was Ptah who created the world through his intelligence and by his spoken word (this anticipated the Greek doctrine of the divine *logos*). Ptah was considered by his priests to be the ultimate creative force behind the actions of the other creator gods, including Atum and the Ennead of Heliopolis. He was the foundation of all wisdom, morals, cities, and people. He was the originator of abstract as well as material qualities. These were concepts that many Egyptians found difficult to handle. In due course, Ptah was joined to Osiris and became an influence on the afterlife.

Below: The souls of the dead are weighed by the jackal-headed god, Anubis, to determine their worth, and watched by the devourer, Amemait, who stands ready to snatch up those who are found to be unworthy.

Thebes

The creation myth of Thebes came later in the New Kingdom because the priests of Amon (originally associated with the creation myth of Hermopolis) wanted to raise

the status of their god. Thebes, they maintained, was the Primeval Mound—the site of watery chaos and where Amon first created himself. All other gods were manifestations of him. He was also Ptah. He was the lotus from which creation grew. He was the Ogdoad, and he became the Primeval Mound of Memphis. Thebes took over the creation myth of Heliopolis and claimed that Osiris was born in the New Kingdom capital.

Above: Anubis and Amemait weigh the souls of the dead in the Judgment Halls of Osiris. The Egyptians believed that they had a fair chance to argue their cases for entering the afterlife, but that their misdeeds would count against them.

Gods of Birth and Death

Birth, death, and the afterlife were of great importance to the ancient Egyptians. Passages from one world to the next were overseen by a hierarchy of gods and goddesses, each with a specific duty.

Tauret

The goddess of childbirth, Tauret was worshiped in Thebes under the New Kingdom. Families often named their children after her and used images of her to

Overleaf: The great constructions and statues of ancient Egypt bolstered the power of the state, whose firm control and confidence was essential to holding together the straggling length of civilization along the Nile.

Above: The jackal-headed Anubis supporting the mummy of Hunefer in the land of the dead, attended by his mourning wife and daughter, with priests. The family made offerings of food to sustain the dead relation.

Opposite: A hand-colored mezzotint depicting the suicide of Cleopatra, from a mid-nineteenth-century edition of Shakespeare's works. The ancient Egyptians have provided a fund of images and tales for subsequent generations.

decorate their homes. She was portrayed as a hippopotamus, standing on her back legs with drooping breasts. Sometimes she was shown as a goddess of vengeance as a hippopotamus with the head of a lion, brandishing a dagger.

Heket

Another protector of women in childbirth, Heket was represented as a frog or frog-headed woman, and was associated with the flooding of the Nile. Some said that she emerged from the mouth of Ra and that she was one of the midwives who helped give birth to the sun each morning.

Meskhet

Another goddess of childbirth, Meskhet was represented by a head placed on the two bricks Egyptian mothers crouched on when they gave birth. She wore two

Above: A Bedouin camel driver passes the main pyramids at Giza. Their secrets may have been plundered but they have lost none of their presence.

palm shoots on her head, and was similar to a fairy godmother who appeared at the birth of a child and predicted its future. She also appeared at the other end of life, when she pleaded before the judgment of Osiris on behalf of the dead.

Shai

Together with seven other gods each named Hather, Shai was regarded as the god of destiny who decreed the fate of individuals when they were born and stood beside them at their final trial to render an account of their lives.

Renenet

More positive in approach than Shai, the goddess Renenet was responsible for the suckling of a baby and often gave the baby its name and determined its personality and good fortune. She was present at the person's death to render an account of that life as well. Sometimes Renenet was portrayed as a woman with the head of a snake or a lioness.

Renpet

Her name meant year, and she was popular as the Egyptian goddess of youth and the coming of spring and fruitfulness. She was represented as a woman wearing a long palm shoot.

Bes

One of the greatest characters among the gods, Bes was extremely popular. Sometimes known as the Lord of Punt, he was an outsider who took on a vital role as the guardian of sleeping and dreaming. As the god of marriage, he presided over the toilet of women and childbirth, and he became a protector of expectant moth-

Left: Nut, the sky goddess, in the form of a cow with a star-spangled belly, being supported by her father Shu and other gods, to separate her from her brother/husband Geb, god of the earth.

ers. His image appeared on bed heads, hand mirrors, and bottles of scent, as he rose steadily from being a friend of the common people to a figure of respect among wealthier Egyptians. He even became a family guardian against threatening beasts such as lions, crocodiles, snakes, and scorpions.

Bes was depicted as a dwarf: stockily built, with a large head, great eyes, an open mouth, protruding tongue, a hairy chin, a stout belly, and bandy legs with his hands on hips. Sometimes he was shown skipping clumsily, playing the harp or tambourine, or holding a dagger in a menacing fashion. He wore a headdress of ostrich feathers and a leopard skin. Unusual for Egyptian portraits, he was shown typically with a full face rather than in profile. He represented the pygmies brought in from outside Egypt, whose antics—both comic and entertaining, and at times disturbingly aggressive—the aristocratic Egyptians of the Old Kingdom greatly enjoyed. Even after the advent of Christianity, Bes survived as a threat to anyone who mocked him.

Selket

The scorpion goddess was shown as a woman wearing a scorpion on her head and seen as a guardian of marriage. She was also a protector of the dead and stood guard in Tutankhamun's tomb.

The Four Sons of Horus

The Four Sons of Horus were appointed by their father to guard the four cardinal points of the compass and to watch over the heart and entrails of Osiris to make sure that he was never hungry or thirsty. Subsequently, they were the official protectors of the viscera of the dead which were taken from the corpse when it was embalmed and placed in four canopic jars, named much later by the Greeks after their hero Canopus.

The stoppers of the jars were shaped like organ's protector, and each of the Four

Right: The Egyptian goddess Isis taught men how to cure disease. This seventeenth-century illustration shows her with the sacred associations culled from Apuleius.

Right: The Egyptian goddess Isis taught men how to cure disease. This seventeenth-century illustration shows her with the sacred associations culled from Apuleius.

Sons of Horus was responsible for one organ. The human-headed god Imsety was responsible for the liver. The lungs were guarded by Hapi, who had the head of a baboon or a dog. The jackal-headed Duamutef protected the stomach and the hawk-headed Qebhsnuf, the intestines.

Ament

The name meant westerner, and the goddess wore an ostrich feather on her head which was an emblem of the Libyans. Because the West was often associated with the dead, Ament was shown emerging from some trees to welcome the dead and offer them bread and water, though other goddesses also performed this function, such as Nut, Hather, or Ma'at.

Ma'at

Represented as a woman wearing an ostrich feather and sometimes with wings attached to her arms, Ma'at was responsible for weighing the hearts of the dead as they waited for judgment. She was the goddess of truth and justice, and the wife of Thoth, the judge of the gods.

For what she represented to the Egyptians—which was the ideal principle of truth and justice—the recognition of the moral correctness and right attitude of the individual, reasonableness, harmony with others and with the forces of life, Ma'at is one of

Left: Falcons at the Temple of Horus in Edfu.

Overleaf: Isis had her own popular cult and temples built in her honor. This is the Philae Temple at Aswan, the famous temple structure behind the main temple of Isis built by the Roman emperor Trajan.

Above: The hawk-headed Horus and the jackal-headed Anubis take an Egyptian in hand, the one god to protect him, the other to lead him to judgment.

Opposite: The goddess Hather offers the menat, or necklace, as a symbol of healing to Set I. She carries the sun between her horns. (From a painting in his tomb.)

the most interesting of the gods. All Egyptians aspired to ma'at, which they regarded as a moral concept, and the goddess and her statues symbolized this aspiration.

The Judgment Halls of Osiris

When the dead had been wrapped as a mummies, bearing certain talismans and passwords from the *Book of the Dead*, it was assumed that they crossed the fearful space between the land of the living and the kingdom of the dead—the Underworld (known as Tuat), where Osiris sat in judgment on all souls. The deceased person was brought into the Hall of Double Justice by Anubis or Horus. At the end of this immense room sat Osiris. In the center of room, there was a huge set of scales, beside which Ma'at stood to weigh the hearts of the dead. Beside the scales, the monster Amemait (the devourer) also sat. He was a cross between a lion, a hippopotamus, and a crocodile, and he sat waiting to devour the hearts of those who were judged guilty. Forty-two judges sat around the hall, wearing winding sheets, each holding a sharp sword and each with the head of a human or animal. These judges represented the provinces of Egypt and each was responsible for

FROM THE TOMBS OF THE KINGS AT THEBES, DISCOVERED BY G. BELZONI.

London Publifhed by J. Murray 1820.

sizing up some aspect of the deceased's conscience.

The dead person was allowed to argue his case before the judges, by reciting declarations of innocence or negative confession. While he pleaded his case, his heart was weighed against the feather of Ma'at (the symbol of righteousness). The god Thoth then recorded the result. If the scales did not balance, the deceased was fed to Amemait. But if the balance was correct, Osiris welcomed the dead person and invited him to enjoy a life of eternal happiness with the gods and the spirits of other dead people.

There were a number of tasks the dead had to perform—such as clearing out dikes and canals—to keep the kingdom of Osiris in order. However, these duties were delegated to the shabtis or ushabtis (also known as the answerers), which were little statuettes buried with the deceased precisely for this purpose.

Above: Sebek, the crocodile god and god of the Faiyum. A living crocodile was kept in the sacred lake near the city of Crocodopolis as an incarnation of the god.

In all these rituals and in others, there was a sense of personal responsibility that the Egyptians valued greatly. Individuals were accepted into Osiris' kingdom on the basis of their actions among the living. The element of bargaining and arguing the personal case gave people some hope that they might be accepted into the other world even if they transgressed in this one.

The Negative Confession

There was a formal recitation that the dead were supposed to make when they faced their judges. It was no doubt learned by heart in life to be word perfect to improve the chances of the dead to enter the other world. The confession gives a fascinating insight into the moral criteria of the Egyptians: "I have not given short measure... I have not caused any to hunger... I have not taken milk from the mouths of babes... I have not dammed flowing water... ." These are only a handful of the denials. Others in the list include denials of having stolen, eavesdropped, told lies, slandered, or slept with another man's wife.

Sacred Animals

A number of creatures were held to be sacred by the Egyptians and we have already seen that most of the gods either took animal form or possessed the head of an animal in order to distinguish and imbue themselves with certain characteristics.

The best known of the sacred animals was the bull Apis, who lived at Memphis and was regarded as a reincarnation of the god Ptah. Ptah had originally existed as celestial fire. In that form, he made pregnant a heifer which gave birth to Ptah himself in the form of a black bull who had specific marks—a white triangle on his forehead, a vulture with outstretched wings on his back, a crescent moon on one flank, and a scarab on his tongue. The bull was tended to dutifully in the temple at Memphis and allowed out once a day for public viewing. Not only was this a popular tourist attraction, but the movements and behavior of the bull were believed to foretell the future. If Apis did not die of old age but became embarrassingly senile, he was sometimes drowned. There was tremendous mourning on his death and a

Left: Min was a god of desert travel and also of fertility and harvests. He is often depicted holding a flail and with a plumed crown. There were great celebrations on his feast day.

celebration at the announcement of his successor. Some of the mummified bodies of previous reincarnations were discovered at Saqqarah.

Petesuchos (the sacred crocodile) was a reincarnation of the god Sebek, who had his sanctuary in Crocodopolis where he lived in a lake with his sacred family. Visitors who came to see him brought magnificent offerings of food which (when he came to the shore) were placed in his mouth as his jaws were held open.

Several other animals were sacred all over Egypt, such as the cat sacred to the god Bast, the falcon and ibis sacred to Horus or Thoth, and the ram. It was a criminal offense to kill sacred animals. Problems occurred where certain animals were only sacred to local gods and therefore might be protected locally, but were hunted by their neighbors.

Among other animals sacred to certain gods were the cow associated with Hather, the dog-faced ape with Hapi, the frog with Heket, the hippopotamus with Tauret, the jackal with Anubis, the lion with Nefertum and the lioness with Sekhmet and Tefnut, the ram with curved horns with Amon and the ram with wavy horns with Khnum, the scarab with Khepri, the scorpion with Selket, the serpent with Buto, the vulture with Nekhbet, the wolf with Upuaut, and the mythical typhon with Set.

Opposite: Tauret was the goddess of childbirth and took the form of a hippopotamus standing on her back legs.

Below: The goddess Ma'at with her protective wings. She was the goddess of truth and justice, and symbolized moral correctness and harmony with others.

Chapter Three
The Gods & Goddesses

I n addition to those who presided over life and death, a league of gods and goddesses oversaw virtually every aspect of life. And, as with all mythological/religious systems, the aspects and legends of the gods provided a set of moral and spiritual instructions for their mortal worshipers.

Atum

Atum's name has its root in two opposite meanings (not to be and to be complete), which explain his crucial position in Egyptian mythology. This signified that Atum existed during creation. Indeed, he was the "Creator." He was the most ancient god of Heliopolis, and many of his characteristics were later absorbed by other gods as they rose in importance.

The followers of Atum believed that he existed without form inside the great ocean, Nun, and contained within himself all existence. When Atum emerged from the ocean, he produced from himself all other gods, men, and creatures. When he became linked to the sun, he was known as Atum-Ra.

Atum was represented as a man, wearing the double crown of the pharaohs. Sometimes he appeared as a mongoose. He personified both the setting sun and the sun before it rose in the morning.

Ra

Ra (also Re) was the great sun god of the Egyptians, whose cult was based at Heliopolis. Bearing the name Atum, he came from the bosom of Nun, the primordial ocean. In one tale he rose from an egg; in another, from a lotus flower, lifting its head from the ocean. He gave birth entirely on his own to Shu and Tefnut, whose children were Geb and Nut, who in turn gave birth to Osiris, Isis, Set, and Nephthys. Together, these nine make up the divine Ennead of Heliopolis.

Ra governed the land from the prince's palace in Heliopolis, where each morning after his bath and breakfast he would set out in his boat with his scribe to visit the twelve provinces of his kingdom, spending an hour in each one. This voyage symbolized the sun passing across the sky. Ra took different guises at different times of day. At night he was Atum, featured as a human with a double crown; at dawn he was Khepri, the sacred beetle; at noon he was Ra, a man with the head of a falcon crowned by the cobra wrapped around a solar disc (in that guise, he was also associated with Horus and known as Ra-Harakhte or Re'- Horakhty). Some

Opposite: Statue of the young pharaoh Tutankhamun from the Temple of Amon, at Karnak. Despite his youth, in death he was given all the respect and riches that were his due as the king-god of Egypt.

Right: The X-ray of the skull of a mummy of the Ptolemaic period. The mummy is that of a young girl who died of an accident in which her head was crushed and her thighs were pushed into her pelvis.

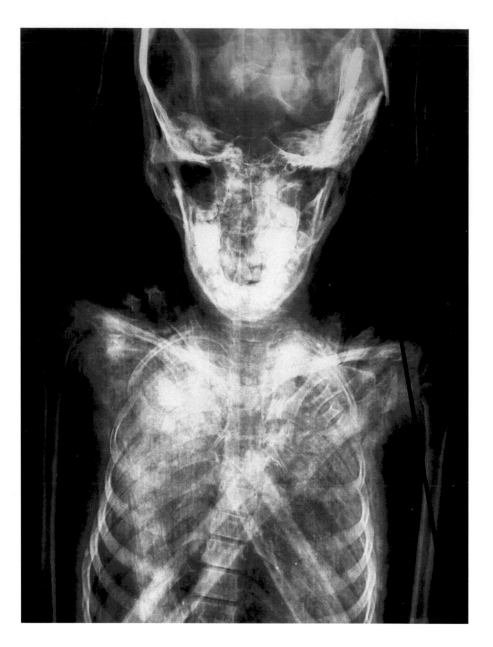

believed that he was born each morning as a child, that he grew during the day into a man, and in the evening declined into old age and death. There were thought to be at least seventy-five different forms and names of Ra.

So long as he was young and vigorous, Ra ruled his kingdom well. When he became old and weak with a trembling mouth and dribbling saliva (some of the greatest pharaohs recognized these debilitating symptoms), the gods and mortal men plotted against him. When Ra learned of their plots, he consulted his advisers. Finally, he threw his divine Eye against his enemies. The Eye, in the form of the goddess Hather, slaughtered the guilty without pity until Ra himself put an end to the massacre before everyone was exterminated. The Eye of Ra, along with the Eye of Horus, became important symbols to the Egyptians. Each month the Eye of Ra was restored by the god Thoth through the waxing and waning of the moon.

Exhausted and disillusioned by these events, Ra wished to withdraw from the world. The goddess Nut was ordered by Nun to change herself into a cow and take Ra on her back into the heavens. This placing of the sun into the sky helped to create the world for humans.

Ra then adopted his fixed routine. He rode his boat across the heavens from east to

west for the twelve hours of daylight, and during the twelve hours of darkness he went through the caverns of the underworld bringing light to its miserable inhabitants. During the day, he had to avoid his great enemy Apep (a serpent who lived in the depths of the celestial Nile), who sought to swallow Ra's boat during a total eclipse.

Ra was worshiped as the creator and ruler of the world. From the time of the Old Kingdom, the pharaohs revered Ra and associated themselves with him. They called themselves the sons of Ra and assumed all the powers of Ra. The pharaohs fostered this belief throughout Egyptian history, until the time of Alexander the Great. Ra himself was thought to lie with the queen at the conception of each new pharaoh, and so he became the god of the living just as Osiris became the god of the dead.

Above: Workers uncovering the entrance of the false passage in the pyramid of Chephren. In most cases, traps and false passages failed to deter the tomb robbers who greedily disturbed the pharaohs' eternal peace.

Shu and Tefnut

Twin brother and sister, they were the first gods to be created by Ra on his own. The word shu means raise or hold up, and it was Shu who held up the sky. He was also god of the air. He was represented in human form with an ostrich feather, an ideogram of his name.

When Ra withdrew from the world, Shu succeeded him as ruler. Just like his father, he was attacked by the children of the serpent Apep. He suffered the plotting of his followers as well. When he became old and diseased, he abdicated his throne in favor of his son Geb, and withdrew into the skies during a terrible storm.

Shu and Tefnut gave birth to Geb (the earth god) and Nut (goddess of the sky). Angered by the secret marriage of Geb and Nut, Ra ordered Shu to slip between them to separate them, so that Nut was raised high into the air where she remained supported by the arms of Shu.

Left: The great Sphinx at Giza is 150 feet long and 75 feet high at the top of its head. It is in the form of a lion with the head of a human. At Karnak, there is a more unusual avenue of ram-headed sphinxes.

Shu's twin sister and consort, Tefnut, was shown as a lioness or as a woman with the head of a lion. She was goddess of the dew and rain. Between them, they represented the space between heaven and earth.

Anhur

Closely identified with Shu, Anhur was often worshiped under the name Anhur-Shu yet he had special characteristics of his own. He symbolized the creative power of the sun and the creative energy of humans. He was sometimes regarded as a

warlike manifestation of Ra. The Greeks saw him as the god of battle, and he was represented wearing a long robe, the headdress of a warrior, with four tall feathers, and carrying a lance.

Anhur became very popular during the New Kingdom and was worshiped as the savior and the good warrior. Soldiers called on his help against their enemies and to protect them against the poisonous creatures he hunted down. His festivals were great occasions for mock battles.

Geb and Nut

God of the earth and goddess of the sky, these siblings were the children of Shu and Tefnut, and the parents of Osiris, Isis, Set, and Nephthys. At first they were closely united but were separated by their father Shu. After this separation Geb lay under Shu's feet, grieving for his wife. He was propped on one elbow with one knee bent to represent the mountains and valleys. His tears of grief produced the world's oceans and seas. Geb was usually represented as a man but sometimes he was associated with a goose and was known as the Great Cackler. As the parents of Osiris, Geb and Nut were also known as the Father and Mother of the Gods.

Geb succeeded Shu to the throne as the third divine pharaoh. One story told how Geb ordered the golden box containing Ra's uraeus (headpiece) to be opened. Inside was the divine snake which killed Geb's companions and seriously injured Geb himself, who was only cured by a lock of Ra's hair which was kept in the same fortress as the golden box. When he recovered, Geb ruled his kingdom well. Eventually he retired to heaven, like Ra and Shu, and left the throne to his son Osiris. In heaven, he replaced Thoth as Ra's herald and became the arbiter of disputes among the gods.

Nut had married her twin brother Geb secretly and against the wishes of Ra. When Ra ordered Shu to separate them, he also commanded that Nut could not bear a child in any month of any year. Thoth took pity on Nut and won five additional days (beyond the 360 official calendar days), while playing draughts with the Moon. During those five days, Nut was able to give birth to her children, Osiris, Set, Isis, and Nephthys, and a fifth child, Horus the Older (Haroeris).

Nut is depicted as a woman with an elongated body and a star-spangled belly arched over the heavens, touching the earth with her toes and fingertips. She is sometimes shown as a cow, or with a rounded vase on her head. The vase is an ideogram of her name. She became the guardian of the dead and was often shown holding the deceased. On the inner lid of sarcophagi, her image was stretched above the mummy.

Left: The funeral of a pharaoh, with the weighing of the soul, beneath, in the Judgment Hall of Osiris. Offerings lie beside the coffin that contains the mummy of the pharaoh.

Below: The entrance to the pyramid of Chephren (or Khafra), built in the fourth dynasty. This print is from the nineteenth century, when exploration of ancient Egyptian sites became very popular.

Osiris

Osiris became the most important god of the Heliopolis cycle, or Ennead. The Greek historian Plutarch wrote a description of his story so that we know more about him than about any other god. Osiris was the first son of Geb and Nut. He was born at Thebes in Upper Egypt first amid loud rejoicing and then much weeping when it was known what problems he would encounter. His great grandfather Ra willingly accepted Osiris as his heir, despite the curse that Ra had put on Osiris' mother, Nut.

The god was handsome and tall. When Geb retired to the heavens, Osiris succeeded him as king of Egypt and his sister, Isis, became his queen. He immediately set about improving the life of his people. He abolished cannibalism, taught people how to make agricultural implements and how to produce grain and grapes for bread, wine, and beer. He built towns, established laws, and started the cult of the gods by building the first temples, creating the first statues and images of the gods, and inventing flutes for religious music.

He then set out on the peaceful conquest of Asia, determined to spread the benefits of his rule to people outside Egypt. He left Isis as regent in his absence, and took with him Thoth, his grand vizier, Anubis, and Upuaut. He traveled throughout the world winning over the countries he visited by music and sheer personal goodness. On his return, he found that Isis had kept excellent order.

But his return upset their brother, Set, who was jealous of the power and success of Osiris and organized a plot against him, hoping to seize the throne. Taking advantage of the festivities that marked the return of Osiris to Egypt, Set invited his brother to a banquet during which he produced a magnificent coffer which he jestingly explained should belong to the god who would fit into it. Osiris agreed to try it out and was immediately imprisoned by Set's accomplices who battened down the lid and threw the coffer into the Nile. It drifted out to sea and across to Byblos on the Phoenician coast, where it came to rest at the foot of a tamarisk tree

that grew with such speed that the coffer became tightly encased within its trunk. Not knowing about the coffer, the king of Byblos ordered the tree to be used as a support for his palace. When it was cut down it gave off the most marvelous scent. The rumor of this marvel spread rapidly and widely.

The rumor reached the ears of Isis, who in great distress had been searching for her brother since Set's assassination attempt. She recognized the meaning of the story, traveled quickly to Phoenicia, and persuaded the king to give her the tree trunk. She freed the coffer from the wood, bathed it in tears, and took it back to Egypt where she hid it in the swamps of Buto. While hunting by moonlight in the swamps of the delta, Set came across the coffer by chance and ordered the body of Osiris to be cut into fourteen pieces and spread throughout the land. This cruelty angered many of the gods and even Set's wife, Nephthys, left him to join Isis and her followers.

For a long time, Isis searched diligently and discovered all but one of the pieces of Osiris' body. The missing piece was the phallus which had been eaten by the greedy Nile crab, the Oxyrhynchid. In consequence of which, the crab became a cursed creature ever afterwards. Isis put the rest of Osiris together again and, with the help of her nephew Anubis, the grand vizier Thoth, and Horus (the Younger, the son she conceived with the miraculously revived body of her husband Osiris while it lay in hiding in the swamp), she carried out the first act of embalming which restored Osiris to eternal life.

Her work done, Isis then hid in the swamps of Buto to avoid Set's anger and to bring up her son Horus until he was old enough to take revenge on his father's murderer.

Isis

From her origins as a minor god of the Delta, Isis (whose name means the seat) grew in importance for the Egyptians and absorbed many of the attributes of other goddesses. She became the wife of Osiris, the god of a nearby town, and the

Above: Bas-relief of various gods and pharaohs on the facade of the funeral temple of Hapsheput, near Luxor.

Above: Anubis receives gifts from a recently deceased Egyptian. Everything possible was done to ease the passage of the dead to eternal life.

Osirian legend was built around them—as brother and sister and as co-rulers. She helped Osiris bring civilization to Egypt by teaching the women to grind corn, spin flax, and weave cloth. She taught the men how to cure disease. She also encouraged men and women to marry and live domestic lives.

Isis ruled Egypt alone while Osiris was on his world tour of peaceful conquest. When their brother Set killed Osiris, Isis recovered his body and bore their son Horus, who grew up to avenge his father with the help of his mother's magic powers that could overcome all the dangers that beset him.

Isis had a reputation as a sorcerer and sometimes used her skills mischievously. Before her marriage to Osiris, she persuaded Ra (whom she served), to tell her his secret name. Ra was an old man at the time and Isis used some earth moistened by his spittle to make a poisonous snake that bit Ra severely. Ra then had to beg Isis to use her spells to cure him but she would not do so until he told her his name. When he did, the name passed directly into Isis, giving her further powers which she vowed to dedicate to the benefit of mankind.

Isis represented the rich plains of Egypt which were fertilized by the annual flooding of the Nile in the form of Osiris. Isis and Osiris were separated from each other by their brother Set, who represented the desert. Isis was worshiped widely in Egypt and she was popular well into Greek and Roman times when she also became the guardian of travelers. There were oftentimes great festivals and processions in her honor. She was much loved by the Egyptians, and represented all manner of excellent virtues such as selflessness, loyalty, honor, and courage.

Isis was represented with a throne on her head, which was an ideogram of her name but also with a disc set between cows' horns and sometimes with two feathers on either side. At times, she bore a cow's head on a human body. The cow drew a link between Isis and Hather. As a guardian of the dead, Isis had winged arms with which to protect them.

Set

The evil brother of Isis and Osiris tore himself from the womb of Nut and was covered in red hair like an ass. Jealous of Osiris, he tricked him into a box which he threw into the Nile. When it was recovered by Isis, Set cut Osiris' body into pieces. This murder was eventually avenged by Horus, the son of Isis and Osiris, and the gods banished Set to the desert.

Set represented the spirit of evil and destruction, the arid desert, drought and darkness, and was in opposition to the spirit of good, of light, and fertility, all of which were represented by Osiris. This conflict between the gods may have had a historical basis. Set represented the Lord of Upper Egypt who was defeated by the worshipers of the falcon god. At first, Set was not regarded so badly: The Hyksos rulers identified him with their own god Sutekh and built a temple to honor him. Ramesses II, during the New Kingdom, called himself the beloved of Set. However, Set was increasingly opposed by the followers of Osiris and from the tenth century B.C. onwards, images of Set were destroyed and his name was eradicated.

Set was associated with many desert animals and also with the hippopotamus, crocodile, boar, and scorpion. He took the mythical form of a fantastic beast with a thin, curved snout, straight, square ears, and a stiff-forked tail. The Greeks called this animal a typhon. Sometimes Set is shown as a human with the head of the typhon.

Horus (the Younger)

Horus, the son of Isis and Osiris, was known by the Greeks as Harsiesis. It was important to distinguish him from other gods also called Horus, especially Horus the Elder (a sun god with the head of a falcon), who represented the sky.

Horus the Younger was conceived by Isis out of the dead body of her husband Osiris. He was often represented as a naked baby, adorned only with jewelry. He had a shaven head, except for one lock of hair that fell onto one side of his temple. He was often pictured seated on his mother's lap, taking milk from her breast. Brought up in secrecy (for fear of being murdered by Set like his father Osiris), Horus was a weak child and only saved from a number of potential disasters by the magical powers of his mother. He was bitten by savage beasts and stung by scorpions. He was burnt and suffered acute stomach pains. Later, he became associated with cures for these ailments. Osiris sent Thoth to help Horus recover from the serpent's poisoning by reciting the cosmic disasters that would occur if Horus did not recover. When he grew up Horus took sanctuary with the people of the delta and became their leader, as they planned out how they would get the better of his evil uncle Set.

Below: Bas-relief of the god Horus the Elder, at his temple in Edfu.

Above: The sacred pool alongside the temple of Amon-Ra at Karnak. The Temple started as a simple shrine, but grew over two thousand years to cover 250 acres.

When Isis finally used her magic powers to call on Osiris to help their son, Osiris appeared in a vision and advised Horus how to defeat Set. Despite following the advice and after some fierce encounters between Horus and the followers of Set—in which they attempted to hide in the bodies of animals such as hippopotami and crocodiles—Horus was unable to overcome his enemy. The tribunal of the gods decided it was time to make their own judgment and summoned the protagonists before them. Set claimed that Horus was illegitimate but Horus proved Osiris was indeed his father. Set was condemned and Horus became the ruler of the two Egypts, reasserted the authority of Osiris throughout the land, and reigned peacefully for many years. He became the national god of Egypt and was regarded as the ancestor of the pharaohs.

Hather

One of Egypt's most ancient and revered goddesses, Hather was a sky goddess and the wife or mother—depending on the particular myth—of Horus the Elder (the sky god). She was also known as the daughter or mother of Ra, and carried the sun between her horns. Her name meant the temple of Horus and one myth related that Horus entered her mouth each evening to rest and re-emerged each morning. She was represented as a cow, which was her sacred animal, or as a woman with horns or with cows' ears.

Her favorite musical instrument was the sistrum, which she played to drive away evil spirits. The sistrum had a small frame on the end of a short handle. Across the frame were strung metal discs that rattled when the instrument was shaken. The head of the goddess was often part of the instrument's design.

Right: Anubis was responsible for laying out and preparing the mummy. He first invented the mortuary rites at the death of Osiris, and became known as "Lord of the Mummy Wrappings."

Below: The good cow goddess Hather carrying the dead man and his soul. Among her other duties, Hather was also known as the "Queen of the West," and was the protectress of the necropolis regions of the Nile.

Hather was the guardian of women. She presided at their toilet. She was also the goddess of joy and love, music, song, dance, and merriment. The living were nourished by suckling the milk from her breasts, and the king especially gained strength from it so that he could perform his duty of protecting Egypt. As Queen of the West, Hather welcomed the dead on their arrival into the other world, and protected the Theban necropolis. Known also as the Lady of the Sycamore, she hid in the sycamores on the edge of the desert to provide bread and water for those who were newly dead and to help them climb the ladder to heaven.

Her most important temple was at Dendera where there were great festivals, particularly on New Year's Day, which was her birthday. Her image was brought out of the temple onto the terrace before dawn so that it would catch the first rays of the rising sun. Later in the day there was much singing, dancing, and drinking. Drinking was always associated with Hather after the time when Ra had supposedly gotten her drunk in order to stop the slaughter he had instructed her to make of those who had plotted against him.

Anubis

Properly known by the Egyptians as Anpu or Anup, Anubis got his name from the Greeks. It was his job to show the dead the way to the other

world. Anubis was represented as a black jackal with a bushy tail, or as a black-skinned man with the head of a jackal or dog. From earliest times, Anubis presided over the embalming of the dead and received funeral prayers from the family of the deceased.

In one text, Anubis is referred to as the fourth son of Ra, and his daughter Kebehut was known as the goddess of freshness. Later, he became part of the Osirian myth and was regarded as the son of Nephthys, who had no children by her husband Set, but conceived Anubis through adultery with her elder brother Osiris. When Nephthys abandoned Anubis at birth, he was found by his aunt Isis who—despite the adultery of her husband Osiris—looked after Anubis and raised him. Everyone seemed satisfied with this arrangement, and Anubis eventually accompanied Osiris on his journey of peaceful conquest around the world. He helped Isis and Nephthys to bury his father when Osiris was murdered and dismembered by Set.

It was Anubis who initiated funeral rites and who embalmed Osiris to protect him from decomposition. He became known as Lord of the Mummy Wrappings and presided over funerals. He received the mummy at the door of the tomb, and then made sure that the funeral offerings were passed on to the deceased. Anubis then took the dead by the hand and led them into the presence of the divine judges before whom he weighed their souls.

Thoth

Worshiped throughout Egypt, Thoth was the god of wisdom and the patron of the scribes in the temple. He was also the patron of science, literature, and inventions. He was the spokesman of the gods and the keeper of their records. Thoth was associated with the moon and was portrayed as a man with the head of an ibis, often

Below: The soul, set free at death, flying out to the sunlight. The Egyptians believed in the certainty of a better life after death if they followed the rules in life.

surmounted by a crescent. Sometimes he was also represented as an ibis itself, or as a baboon or dog-headed ape. The priests of Hermopolis believed that Thoth was the divine ibis who had hatched the egg of all creation, and generated the first four gods and goddesses. They ensured that the sun continued to run its course by singing hymns in the morning and in the evening.

Thoth was regarded at times as the oldest son of Ra, and as such he was believed to take the place of Ra in the sky at night when Ra traversed the underworld. Sometimes he was said to be the child of Geb and Nut, brother of Isis and Osiris, but usually he is known as Osiris' vizier and scribe.

After traveling with Osiris around the world, Thoth helped Isis to restore the murdered Osiris, largely by the purity of his voice in making the magic incantations. He helped Isis protect her child Horus, driving out the poison that infected him from the sting of a scorpion. Later, he helped to cure the wounds of Horus and Set in their long, drawn-out struggle. Finally, he judged between the two enemies, condemned Set to banishment, became vizier to Horus, succeeded Horus to

the throne, and ruled long and peacefully.

Thoth possessed many skills and attributes in the arts and sciences, in arithmetic, astronomy, medicine, magic, music, drawing, and—most importantly—in writing. Writing enabled humanity to record his wisdom for future generations. He was known as the Lord of Holy Words because he invented hieroglyphs. Above all, he was famed for his truthfulness.

Thoth's divine responsibilities were very great. Not only did he control the moon and measured time into months and years, but also he kept the divine archives, recorded the history of the pharaohs, and recorded the judgment of Osiris on the dead brought into his presence. He presided as a judge himself and at coronations of the new pharaoh. There were gifts of honey, figs, and sweetmeats at his festival, which was celebrated shortly after the New Year. His chief wife was Seshat, who had many of the same attributes as her husband. She became the goddess of writing and of history. She was known as the Mistress of the House of Books and as the Mistress of the House of Architects in her capacity as the foundress of temples. One of her busiest tasks was that she recorded the booty won from foreign conquests.

The Book of Thoth, which was believed to record the wisdom of the god himself, was a collection of papyrus rolls with information on the sciences (including astronomy and astrology), religious traditions, regulations concerning the priesthood, and philosophy and medicine. This was essential reading for scholars and scribes. Much of the information was recorded elsewhere and the book itself has never been recovered.

Amon

Amon was the state god of Egypt in the New Kingdom, with temples at Karnak and Luxor in Thebes, in Memphis, and elsewhere. He was portrayed as a ram, or as

Left: A wall painting from a fourth dynasty tomb. It was believed that everyday scenes in the tomb made the deceased feel at home and asserted his achievements in life.

a handsome young man wearing two plumes.

Amon was sometimes known as the King of the Gods. He may have originated in Hermopolis but little is heard of him in the Old Kingdom, until he displaced the god of Thebes and first became prominent there in the twelfth dynasty. He rose to enormous influence during the eighteenth dynasty. Thebes itself became known as Nut Amon (the city of Amon), or simply Nut (the city). The conquering pharaohs who bore the name Amenhotep were the sons of Amon. Like Atum of Heliopolis, Amon was believed to have given birth to himself and to have formed all other gods at the Primeval Mound of Memphis. He also became part of the divine Ogdoad of Hermopolis. Eventually, he retired to the heavens where he dwelt as the god Ra.

Amon was depicted as a handsome young man wearing a crown with two tall feathers. He is also portrayed seated on a throne or standing with a whip raised above his head. Sometimes he had the head of a ram with curled horns. A ram was kept at Karnak as a living incarnation of the god. A goose was also sacred to him.

In the guise of the ram, Amon was seen as the god of fertility and reproduction and the creative power of life that ensured the harvest. He gave the pharaohs victory over their enemies. The pharaohs were believed to be his sons. As Amon-Ra and as Thebes became increasingly powerful, he adopted many of the characteristics and importance of Ra himself. His temple at Thebes received vast wealth through foreign tributes and donations by victorious pharaohs, such as Ahmose and his successors.

Above: A section through the tomb of the pharaoh Seti I clearly shows the elaborate tunnels and chambers created as the last resting place for a wealthy king.

Aten

The great power of Amon caused a reaction during the reign of Amenhotep IV, when the priests of Heliopolis—jealous of the wealth of Thebes—encouraged the pharaoh to reassert the cult of Ra under his name Aten of the day. This challenge was highly successful but only briefly. Amenhotep changed his name to Akhenaton (the glory of Aten) and established a new capital from which he compelled worship of Aten and attacked the temples of Amon.

Aten was symbolized by the disc of the sun. There was never any personification of him in statues or in pictures. He was represented in the form of a great disc from which fanned out the long rays of the sun ending in hands with long finger-

Opposite: The goddess Ma'at and a royal cobra, from the tomb of the pharaoh Seti I. Ma'at, who personified the spirit of Egypt, helped Anubis weigh the souls of the dead.

Above: The Egyptians believed that the endless rays of the sun represented the hands and fingertips of Aten, stretched out either to receive or to offer gifts.

tips, offering or receiving gifts. The only priest of the cult was the pharaoh himself, who also composed the hymns that were sung to Aten in his temple with its vast courtyard and obelisk of the sun. The cult of Aten was an attempt at monotheism in which all men—of whatever country in the empire of Egypt—were considered equal and in which there were no other gods. In particular, every portrayal of Amon was obliterated: statues were broken, inscriptions cut away, and riches taken from the temples of Amon were transferred to the temples of Aten.

This dramatic change of emphasis lasted only for as long as Akhenaton reigned and did great damage to the power of Egypt. The pharaoh was so obsessed with his cult that he did not bother with the administration and protection of his country. Not surprisingly, his successors reacted to his practice and in due course restored Amon to all his former power and glory. Amon became wholly incorporated with Ra.

Under Ramesses III, the temples of Amon-Ra possessed more than 80,000 slaves and more than 400,000 head of cattle. The priests eventually seized the throne itself and turned Thebes into an independent state which, in turn, established its authority over Ethiopia and the desert tribes of Libya. The greatest temples to Amon were at Karnak and Luxor where Amon, his wife Mut, and their son Khons were worshiped together. The festivals that were celebrated there (with singers, dancers, and ritual feasts) occurred also in other parts of Egypt where Amon was popular. Amon's Bark, a gift of the pharaoh Ahmose I after his victories, was a floating temple at Thebes. This temple was covered in gold, filled with rich ornaments, and sailed on the Nile at one of the major festivals.

Khons

Amon's wife Mut (mother) was represented as a woman wearing the headdress of a vulture. Sometimes she took the cat-form of Bast, or the head of a lioness in the form of Sekhet. Amon and Mut were not able to have children. First they adopted Mont (the original Theban god whom they dispossessed), and then Khons, who was represented as a handsome and head-shaven young man with the traditional youthful lock of hair hanging from one temple. He wore a skullcap surmounted by a disc in a crescent moon. Sometimes he was represented with the head of a falcon.

As he grew in popularity, Khons became a god of healing and his help was sought by many from far outside Egypt. He delegated his powers to statues which were incarnations of himself, a form of early franchising that was highly successful. In one instance, he delegated a form of himself in Syria to cure the daughter of a prince, and later appeared to the prince in a dream as a falcon flying toward Egypt. The grateful prince immediately traveled to Egypt to return the statue to Karnak with costly gifts. No doubt the priests of Karnak relished such skillful calling-in of debts.

Below: Seti I was a military commander who expanded the empire. The Ethiopian and Nubian figures painted on the wall of his tomb are reminders of his successes abroad.

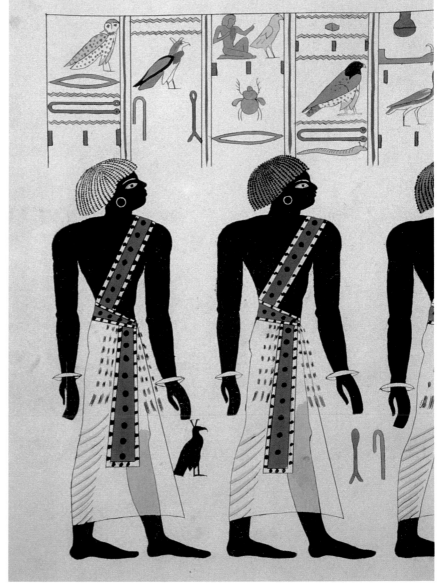

Sebek

The crocodile god was depicted either as a man with the head of a crocodile or as the crocodile itself. He was of particular importance to the pharaohs of the thirteenth dynasty, many of whom were called after the god Sebekhotep (Sebek is satisfied). The cult of Sebek was based in the Faiyum and the city of Crocodilopolis. A living crocodile was kept in a sacred lake near the city, as an incarnation of the god. Its name was Petesuchos (Suchos was Greek for Sebek), which means, "He who belongs to Suchos."

To those who worshiped him, Sebek was yet another form of the father figure who emerged from the primeval water to lay his eggs on the bank in order to give birth to the world. But although Sebek was worshiped in some areas he was ritually slaughtered in others, where he was believed to have helped Set to murder Osiris by allowing Set to hide in the body of a crocodile.

Ptah

Worshiped at Memphis from the earliest times and regarded as the Creator of all things, the source of moral order, and Lord of Truth and Justice, Ptah was shown as a man wrapped as a mummy with his head enclosed in a tight head-band and a large collar around his neck and shoulders. His hands were free, and he held a scepter which combined the emblems of life, stability, and omnipotence.

Sometimes Ptah was represented in a completely different guise, as a dwarf with deformed legs, hands on hips, and a large head with the youthful lock of hair. In this form, he was a powerful protector against certain animals and many evils.

Ptah was of great importance to many of the pharaohs, particularly in the nineteenth dynasty to Seti I and Ramesses II. Subsequently, with the political dominance of the delta region, Ptah rose to widespread influence and wealth. He became almost as important as the great gods Amon and Ra.

He was the patron and protector of artisans and artists, and was regarded as the master builder of the great architectural monuments that first rose in the Old

Above: Hather Temple, Dendera, with the king making an offering to Hather, who is nursing her son, Ihi.

Kingdom. He was famed for various miracles, one of which was to thwart an Assyrian attack led by Senacherib, by summoning an army of rats to gnaw through the bow strings and leather thongs of the enemy shields.

His temple at Memphis was dedicated to Ptah, his consort Sekhmet (the lioness), and to their son Nefertum, who was later replaced by Imhotep (a human hero raised to the status of a god). Ptah was also associated with the bull Apis, who was housed by his temple and was regarded as a living incarnation of the god.

Sekhmet

The partner of the god Ptah at Memphis, Sekhmet was portrayed as a lion or a woman with the head of a lion, and sometimes with a sun disc on her head. She was regarded with awe as a goddess of war and battle. Her name means the powerful. She was also called the beloved of Ptah. Despite her aggressive reputation, she helped to heal bone fractures.

To add confusion, the name Sekhmet was a title given to the goddess Hather when she took the form of a lioness to attack the men who had turned against the god Ra. She slaughtered so many of them and refused to stop when Ra begged her to, that he had to resort to a trick to save the rest of the human race. He mixed a potion of beer and pomegranate juice and spread seven thousand jugfuls across the battlefield. Thinking it was human blood, Sekhmet lapped it up and became so drunk that she could not continue the killing. To avoid any subsequent revenge at his trick, Ra decreed that as many jugs of the potion should be brewed on that same day each year as there were priestesses of the sun. The festival became a time of heavy drinking.

Bast

Bast (or Bastet) was the local goddess of the Lower Egyptian town of Bubastis, which gained in importance—as did the goddess—when it became the capital of the Libyan-dominated kingdom in the twenty-second dynasty. Bast was represented

82

as a cat-headed woman holding a musical instrument in her right hand—usually a sistrum decorated with the figure of a cat—and a basket in her left. Although she also became the wife of Ptah of Memphis, she was very different from Ptah's other wife, the lion goddess Sekhmet.

Bast was primarily a goddess of pleasure, though she was also the guardian of pregnant women and protected men against contagious diseases and evil spirits. She loved music and dance. The festivals in her honor were some of the liveliest celebrated by the Egyptians right up until Roman times. The temple at Bubastis was one of the most elegant in Egypt. According to the Roman historian Herodotus, hundreds of thousands of people came each year by barge, with flutes and castanets to exchange jokes and play tricks on each other while joking with the people on the banks who watched them sail by. There was a great procession through the town and huge quantities of wine were drunk, which greatly increased the popularity of the goddess.

Left: "Cleopatra's Needle" has nothing to do with Queen Cleopatra. It is the obelisk of Thothmes, quarried at Syene, erected at Heliopolis in about 1500 B.C., and shipped to England in the nineteenth century.

Overleaf: Beyond the massive blocks of stone rises the pyramid of Chephren at Giza.

Those who worshiped the cat goddess set up numerous statues of the cat, and large numbers of the mummified bodies of cats were buried near her sanctuaries.

Khnum (with Sati and Anukis)

Represented as a ram-headed man with long wavy horns and a solar disc (in contrast to the curved horns of the god Amon), Khnum was a god of the region of the

Below: The Pyramid of Cheops at Giza stands prominently out of the flat plain. However well-known the image of the pyramids, visitors today never fail to be awed by their size and the ambition that built them.

cataracts and symbolized the River Nile. His sanctuary was on the island of the Elephantine, and he protected the sources of the Nile together with his two wives, Sati and Anukis.

His name meant the molder and he was believed to have shaped the world egg on his potter's wheel and then shaped Osiris and all other living creatures. He was referred to as, "the potter who shaped men and fashioned the gods." He formed children in the womb, particularly the young pharaohs. The Nubian rulers adopted Khnum during the New Kingdom and spread his cult widely.

Sati (one of Khnum's two wives) was also a guardian of the Cataracts. She was armed with a bow and arrows, not only for hunting but also as a means of releasing the force of the river's current. Sati was represented as a woman with the horns of a cow supporting the conical crown of the South.

Anukis was Khnum's second wife, the goddess of the First Cataract of the Nile. She was shown as a woman wearing a plumed crown and carrying a staff. Her name meant the Clasper, representing the tight passage of the river between the rocks.

Min

The Greeks identified Min with their god Pan. He was a very ancient god of Egypt (always represented with an erect penis), who had a flail raised in his right hand behind his head, wearing a crown with two straight feathers. He was associated with the creation of the world and with the god Horus.

Min was worshiped as the protector of travelers in the desert and as the god of roads. His cult was centered at Coptos, which was a major point of departure for caravans across the desert. By contrast with the desert, he was regarded as a god of fertility and a protector of crops and as such he was celebrated with great festivities and with gymnastic games.

Hapi

Representations of Hapi showed individual character that was unusual among the Egyptian gods. He was regarded as the manifestation of the Nile and appeared as a man with a paunch supported by the belt of a fisherman or boatman. He had hanging breasts (more like those of a woman), and a crown of river plants—either the lotus of Upper Egypt or the papyrus of Lower Egypt. His breasts symbolized the fecundity of the river, and he was celebrated in rituals that welcomed the return of the annual floods.

Imhotep

Greatly admired by his contemporaries, Imhotep was one of the very few Egyptians who rose from being a commoner to becoming the king's vizier and eventually achieved the status of a god. He was the great architect who built the oldest surviving pyramids for King Zoser in the third dynasty. Eventually in the New Kingdom, he came to be regarded as a god (the son of Ptah), whose high priest he had been during his life. His greatest achievement was the step pyramid at Saqqarah, which became a symbol of the spiritual aspirations of the Egyptians.

He was represented dressed as priest, with no crown, seated and reading from a scroll. He became the protector of scribes and doctors.

Chapter Four
Egyptian Life

S ince the Egyptians were a highly advanced society blessed with an abundance of natural resources for food and water, they were able to devote time and resources to more artistic and technological pursuits. Their advanced knowledge of engineering, science, and the arts merged with their religious beliefs, all played a role in their everyday lives.

The Land and the People

Upper and Lower Egypt were like two separate countries: the narrow length of the Nile, with arid desert on either side; and the wide delta, which was immensely more fertile in ancient Egyptian days. The Egyptians always preserved their sense of duality, and it is reflected in the characteristics of their many gods and goddesses. Even after these two areas of Egypt were united, they repeatedly broke away from each other in times when there was no strong ruler.

Opposite: The land of Egypt was dominated by the River Nile, along whose banks all Egyptian life congregated. In places the vegetation came close to the river; in other parts, high cliffs rose up from the water.

Below: The Nile cataracts above Aswan. Until the time of the Middle Kingdom, the southern border of Egypt was the First Cataract at Aswan. During the New Kingdom, it extended 600 miles south of Aswan.

A pharaoh was the lord of the two lands and wore a double crown, which combined the white crown of Upper Egypt and the red crown of Lower Egypt. It also bore the head of a cobra, the symbol of the goddess Buto of the delta; and the head of a vulture, the symbol of the goddess Nekhbet from the south. For much of Egyptian history, there were two viziers to govern the country, two treasuries, and two granaries. But the people united in common understanding of their mutual dependence on the waters and floods of the Nile. This dependence brought together an extraordinary range of people and ideas which influenced Egyptian life in one way or another for thousands of years. Some of these people included nomadic tribes, Libyans, Nubians, descendants of central Africa, and the dynastic Egyptians themselves.

Below: The Temple at Abu Simbel, near the second cataract of the Nile. The colossal statues of Ramesses II are almost 65 feet high. There is also a great hall and chambers for the pharaoh's residence within the temple.

Natural Resources

Egypt was blessed with plenty of natural resources and looked to trade more for luxuries than necessities. There was open land for crops and cattle. There were fish and birds and wild game for hunting around the Nile, which also provided the main transport route connecting either end of the country. Mud was used for building and for potting, and papyrus for paper, baskets, and boat building. There was flax for fibers and salt for preserving. Palm trees, acacia, and sycamore were designated for timber, and the ample rock in the cliffs for more solid structures and for statues. There were also mines set up for precious metals such as gold and copper as well.

Travel and Trade

The donkey was the most common form of transport for men and goods by land. Horses were not ridden or used as beasts of burden, because they were kept for use in chariots. Camels were not used until later during the Ptolemaic period. Oxen were occasionally used for heavy loads.

Transport by water was much easier. There were reed rafts or light boats for fishing. These might have had sails but would also have oars or paddles to row against the prevailing wind. Larger wooden ships were used for heavier cargos, and these might be clinker built and might have one or two cabins for shelter which was needed during longer journeys. At least one such boat was more than 140 feet (42 m) long and 20 feet (6 m) in the beam. Boats of this size and even larger were used

Above: The Temple of Luxor, seen from the Nile. Boats were one of the main forms of transport and the most important communication link between north and south.

Overleaf: Sunset in the desert at Giza. The Sphinx and pyramids formed one of the most impressive spectacles in Lower Egypt, in the north of the kingdom.

for ocean voyages down the Red Sea and along the coast. They sailed in the Mediterranean to Cyprus, Crete, and the Aegean Islands.

Ostensibly, the king controlled these voyages and all other trading expeditions by land or sea, provided he was in a position to assert his authority, and there were clearly defined and well-guarded frontier posts. Expeditions for trade were important to his coffers as well as to his authority. As there were no coins until very late in Egyptian history, trade was usually by barter, which was a means of exchanging goods.

Some of the earliest expeditions were to Lebanon. They returned with cedar, pine, and juniper. Other notable findings included Syrian pottery, Libyan olive oil, and ebony, ivory, slaves and ostrich feathers from Nubia. Frankincense and myrrh from the land of Punt (Somaliland) were exchanged with Egyptian copper tools

Left: The pharaoh tightly controlled trade outside Egypt, and much of his wealth came from tribute, such as these slaves and gifts, paid by neighboring countries.

and jewelry. Caravans traveled south—beyond the cataracts of the Nile—bringing back precious stones, animal skins, and incense for the temples. Gifts were exchanged between Egyptian kings and foreign rulers, which ranged from gold and ornamented weapons to pygmies and zoo animals such as bears and elephants.

Above: The measure of a man's wealth was his property and cattle. At times, the priests in the great temples owned almost as many cattle as some of the pharaohs. These bulls belonged to a royal prince whose tomb is at Giza.

Agriculture and Food

The success of agriculture depended on drawing off the waters of the Nile to irrigate as much as possible of the surrounding desert. Once the earliest Egyptians had settled into small communities and begun to grow regular harvests of grain, agriculture was the main occupation of most Egyptians. Both men and women were

Above: Dancing, feasting, and music were popular in ancient Egypt, and religious festivals provided excellent excuses for people to not only enjoy themselves, but to earn credit by worshiping the gods.

employed in farming the land. Trenches were dug to take the water from the Nile to the fields, which were ploughed by oxen. After this process, the soil was broken with hoes. The water was drawn up from the Nile by means of a shaduf, a form of pole balanced at one end by a weighted stone and at the other by a container for the water. Sheep were often let into the field to trample the seeds into the ground. The harvest was cut with sickles. Donkeys and asses pulled the loads, and oxen helped to grind the corn. There are many scenes in tomb decorations of peasant farmers working in the fields. The corn bins were large, domed buildings made of mud with an opening at the top that was reached by a ladder. The grain could be drawn off at the bottom through a trapdoor.

Irrigation was under tight central control because it was of such crucial importance, as was the storage of grain. Harvests were taxed. Priests and government officials made sure that everything was carefully recorded. A strong central government was essential to ensure the administration of a controlled system that gave order to the lives of everyone — though in unequal measure. The most successful temples (and their associated gods and priests) owned

96

Left: A detail from the Book of the Dead, *showing the deceased Anhai in adoration. The female figure (probably a goddess) following behind carries a sistrum.*

large areas of land and became rich on the proceeds.

Bread—grown largely from the cereal emmer—was probably the staple diet of the common Egyptian, together with beans. Fruit and vegetables were grown where water was abundant. There were market gardens and orchards growing figs, grapes, dates, and the dom-palm nut. Later in Egyptian history, there were apples, olives, pomegranates, and watermelons. There were also lentils, lettuce, onions, leeks, radishes, cucumbers, and garlic. Carob pods and honey were used for sweeteners. There was meat—both domestic and wild—for those who could afford it or hunt it, together with fish and game birds. Fish were caught in nets and baskets or speared from the river bank and small boats and rafts. Waterfowl were caught in clap-nets. Pigeons were the most plentiful bird, but there were also abundant flocks of ducks and geese. Vineyards were tightly controlled by the aristocracy. Barley was grown for beer which was extremely popular. All the processes of making beer were shown in pictures in the tombs. There was a variety of red and white wines, labeled with the year and place of origin and sometimes with a classification of quality.

Overleaf: The avenue of sphinxes that guard the entrance to the temple at Karnak. The ram-headed sphinxes are more rare than the one at Giza, which has a lion's body and the head of a man.

Marriage and the Family

For a long time there appears to have been no formal religious or civil marriage ceremony to cement the common cohabitation between men and women, though families had a strong place in Egyptian life. Aristocrats and royalty married more formally to establish successions and alliances. Many kings had several wives. They often married their sisters and then took other wives who bore their children, including the heir to the throne. Divorce was not infrequent and involved sharing out common property.

Family life in general was portrayed as an ideal; family groups appeared happy. Men and women stood equally side by side, often holding hands or with their arms around each other while their children stood close by. Wealthy women could own property but did not hold public office. In a moderately wealthy household, a family could include up to six children who were expected to behave properly and grow up to support their parents in their old age. Children started school from

Opposite: The sistrum was a popular musical instrument associated with the goddess Hather. It had a handle topped by a frame with small metal disks that rattled when the sistrum was shaken.

Left: The papyrus plant used to be common in the Nile valley, though it is now quite rare. The stems were used for writing on. They were cut into thin strips and pasted in two layers on top of each other, horizontally and vertically.

101

Above: The royal vulture from the tomb of Seti I. Nekhbet was the vulture goddess and guardian of Upper Egypt; sometimes she was shown as a woman wearing the white crown of Upper Egypt.

about the age of seven. Young children often went naked and wore their hair in a single lock on one side of their head, as shown also in portrayals of some of the youthful gods. Circumcision was common among the Egyptians for reasons of hygiene, but was usually carried out in adolescence rather than at birth. Dogs, cats, and monkeys were kept as pets, although dogs were also used for hunting. Geese were also kept at many homes to warn families against intruders.

Most of the detail we know about social and family life is about the wealthier people because it comes from their own tombs and wall decorations. Each household would have a considerable staff of servants and slaves who were often prisoners of war but in some instances were able buy their freedom. There were—among other members of a wealthy household—cooks, gardeners, doorkeepers, butlers, nurses, sweepers, and laborers on the land.

The family ate with their fingers. Husband and wife sat together and the children rested on cushions on the floor. Servants waiting on all of them. At banquets there would be music, dancers, and acrobats, or dwarves to amuse the company, and plenty of food and wine or beer.

Entertainment

There were board games such as senet, which was played with 12-14 ivory pieces on an oblong chessboard using dice or knucklebones, and a form of ludo using pins. Children played leap frog and ball games with leather-covered balls. They had whipping tops, rattles, toy weapons, and dolls or animals made of wood or clay.

The Egyptians loved music and dancing to the accompaniment of clapping and singing. Orchestras of several instruments sometimes played at banquets. Musical

Left: An Egyptian pharaoh wearing the double crown of Upper and Lower Egypt. Egypt needed strong central administration to hold the country together; hence the cult of the pharaoh as a god with absolute power.

*Right: Ramesses II, through his conquests and strong admin-
istration, raised the reputation and influence of the pharaoh
at home and abroad, giving Egypt tremendous confidence.*

instruments were buried with the dead to ensure that they could enjoy themselves
in the other world. There were trumpets, harps, drums, flutes, and tambourines.
Later, lutes and lyres were invented together with the goddess Hather's special rat-
tle instrument, the sistrum.

Health and Medicine

With a reasonable diet and plenty of sun, the Egyptians should have been quite
healthy, but they suffered from many complaints, as we can tell from the condition

of the mummy remains and also from their own superstitions. But they did not rely simply on magic, old wives tales, and the goodwill of the gods, though these were all considered to be important. There were comprehensive medical texts that gave advice and suggested treatments or prescriptions. There were also detailed texts on bone surgery. Medical libraries were attached to many of the larger temples, and Egyptian physicians and surgeons had such a renown reputation that they often visited the courts of foreign countries.

They suffered from bad teeth, eye infections from flies, appendicitis, rheumatism, arthritis, gout, tuberculosis, pneumonia, smallpox, and high blood pressure, but do not appear to have suffered from venereal diseases. Their teeth were particularly bad. Some mummies were fitted with bridges and gold teeth. Egyptians owed much of their anatomical knowledge to the practice of mummification, which gave them an excellent opportunity to explore the human body and intestines.

Dress

Living in a warm climate, the Egyptians could dress lightly in cotton or linen. Their styles were simple but evolved over the centuries. A form of kilt was the most common garment worn in the earliest years either to the knee or full length, and some-

Below: An Egyptian pharaoh, possibly Ramesses II, carried in triumph after a military victory. Foreign conquests added immensely to the pharaoh's prestige as well as his coffers.

times had a flap at the front. A simple loincloth was worn by many.

The classic woman's garment was a long, sheathlike skirt either white or brightly colored, with shoulder straps that hung from just below the breasts. Well-dressed men wore a large collar of beads that hung over their chests. Women wore beads at their necks, on their wrists, and on their ankles. Hair was cut short and wigs were worn by both men and women, and these hairpieces became fuller as time progressed.

The New Kingdom became much more fashion conscious among the well-to-do. Decorations, belts, capes and pleated blouses were introduced, with jewelry and adornments for the wig which became longer and much more elaborate for women.

Houses and Furniture

The earliest Egyptians lived in one-room houses that were not much more than shelters made of mud, or had walls with a mixture of reed and mud and a reed roof. This developed into a rectangular house which by the time of the Middle

Kingdom might have several rooms and a courtyard within the outer door might include steps leading up to a flat, mud roof where the corn bin might be kept safe from animals. Most people had only a two-room house but the wealthiest had villas with gardens and a large variety of plants.

In the center of the town, houses were close together. In the suburbs they were spread well apart, with some having bathrooms and lavatories with stone seats resting on brick containers filled with sand and wells for fresh water. Royal palaces—though built of much the same material—had rooms which were more spacious with richly colored walls that often had scenes painted on them.

Chairs (often with high backs), tables, and beds were luxuries of the wealthier people. There were some hinged chairs as well, that were collapsible for transporting. Most people sat on the floor or slept on a mat or raised platform. Instead of pillows there were curved headrests made of wood, stone, or pottery, often shaped to a particular person's requirements.

Arts and Crafts

From long before the first dynasty, carved spoons and combs of ivory, copper beads, jewelry made from hard stones, and little statuettes have been found. During the Old Kingdom, we know from the evidence in the tombs that art developed greatly. Gold and copper were used plentifully. There were delicate vases of alabaster, and the typical blue glaze of Egyptian faïence. There was a sophisticated

Above: A lively illustration of an officiating priest attempting to lasso a bull for sacrifice at a religious ceremony.

Opposite: The temple at Karnak, with one of the ram sphinxes that form its entrance.

Overleaf: The temple at Karnak is a series of huge buildings collected together on a vast site and built over a long period of time. The whole complex demonstrates the Egyptians' supreme belief in continuity.

Above: Various images of the goddess Ma'at, with protective wings, decorating the tomb of Set I.

Opposite: The Great Hall at Karnak with its vast pillars. Once richly decorated, it provides remarkable insight into the psyche of the Egyptian pharaohs.

range of tools for carving and this made possible the artifacts and buildings that were energetically produced during the Old Kingdom. Some of the best works of art from this period are the reliefs, which were originally brightly painted in private tombs showing the everyday life of the deceased. There were lifelike statues that were made to replace the body of the deceased if it should decay.

The period of some of the best jewelry was in the twelfth dynasty, during the Middle Kingdom. Some of the work is beautifully intricate and well balanced. Twisted gold wire, lapis lazuli, amethyst, alabaster, and many other materials were used to create ornaments and highly attractive little bowls and figures that often had flower decorations on them. The tomb of Tutankhamun revealed some of the best evidence we have for the richest Egyptian decoration. Some of the most realistic sculptures came during the period of the heretic king Akhenaten, who rejected the god Ra and tried to establish a new state religion.

In time, sculptures became almost too grand and artifacts too elaborate, though there were revivals of good taste. The best of Egyptian art was when it captured delicate detail with deftness and restraint, or brought form to life and energy into its images. Like the art of any time, it was always more successful when the artist seemed to care about what he was doing rather than when he used his craft simply for ostentatious display, which invariably had more of a political or propaganda purpose than an artistic one.

The stylistic representation of the human form in reliefs and in painting is interesting. There were formal guidelines which laid down what was known as the "Canon of the Human Form": Any portraiture was divided into a set number of squares that determined the proportions of the figure. The head was always in profile with the eye shown in full. Shoulders and torso faced the front so that both

arms and hands could be seen clearly. From the armpit down to the stomach and the legs, the figure was in profile again, though the navel was invariably shown in full on the edge of the stomach. One leg was usually slightly in advance of the other. The range of expression in the body and the features that artists achieved within this strict formula was remarkable and so was the durability of this form through so many generations. Gods and men were treated alike, which helped to bring Egyptians closer to their gods.

Literature

Like the literature of most ancient peoples, that of the early Egyptians usually had a moral or didactic purpose. It was intended to instruct people with what to do, how

Below: In a scene typical of the majesty of the ancient land, bare rock and water merge with the art of Egyptian sculpture and engineering at Abu Simbel.

to behave, and what to believe. There were religious texts, texts for the priesthood, and school texts. In due course, there were also tales of adventure, poems of love, popular stories, prayers and songs.

Above: Camels and their riders pass by the pyramids at Giza, painting a perfect picture of serenity.

Most religious texts were specifically intended to increase the reputation of a particular god or—by association—a particular ruler. Texts were copied by scribes down through the generations with modifications that laid emphasis on, or shifted the focus of, the god or ruler as required. The most famous religious text that has survived is the *Book of the Dead*, dated from about 2000 B.C. It is full of spells and incantations that the dead might recite to win themselves a place in the other world.

To win themselves favor in this world, there were a number of texts of maxims and instructions that laid down the proper way to behave in public, or to treat one's elders. One of these texts was written by Ptahhotep—a learned Egyptian of the fifth dynasty—whose maxims were intended for royalty, aristocrats, and ordinary people alike.

Popular stories included the "Eloquent Peasant," which complained about injustice; the "Story of the Shipwrecked Sailor," a Sinbad-type story about a sailor who finds himself a castaway on an island in the Red Sea along with a serpent monster; the "Legend of the Doomed Prince," who tried to avoid his fate to die by the crocodile, the snake, or the dog; the "Story of King Khufu and the Magician," which is full of adventures at a royal court with magical happenings, along the lines of a fairy story with political undertones; and the "Tale of Sinuhe," about a fugitive from

an Egyptian court who managed to slip past frontier guards and took sanctuary in Palestine until in old age he wrote to the pharaoh to beg a pardon so that he could return home before he died. His wish was granted and the tale ended happily.

Love poems and songs, particularly from the Middle and New Kingdoms, were full of separated lovers and sweethearts with invocations to nature and animals to befriend the lovers. The tone of most of these poems was happy and optimistic, though some bemoan the sad or lovelorn fate of the poet.

Science and the Calendar

The Egyptians watched the stars and the action of the moon and the sun, and determined time by their observations. However, they do not appear to have

Left: Hieroglyphs from the tomb of Seti I still glow with amazing color as they tell their encoded story of the rule of this extraordinary pharaoh.

Opposite: Archaeologists remove what the grave robbers failed to find, as the treasures are uncovered from the tomb of Tutankhamun.

thought about the actual construction or nature of celestial bodies in a scientific way. They divided the day and night into twelve hours each, which gave us our own twenty-four-hour clock. At a very early stage in their history, they also developed a calendar of twelve months which had thirty days. When they realized that this was inaccurate, they added five extra days to each year, which was reflected in their mythology. Instead of four seasons they had only three seasons which were determined by the demands of agriculture: there was akhet, when the floods came; peret, when the floods receded; and shemu, when the harvest came. They measured time by a shadow clock or sundial during the day, or by water clocks which allowed water to drip out in a measured time through a hole at the bottom of a bowl. Neither of these methods were very accurate.

Mathematic calculations were long-winded, though in this case their measurements were extremely accurate because they had to be for the remarkable construction of the pyramids. They used a decimal system with different signs for units, tens, hundreds, thousands and so on. The necessary number of signs had to be added up to reach the total of any number. To multiply anything, they had to double it several times and then add the signs for whatever was left over. It was surprisingly cumbersome for a people who had cracked so many other technical problems.

Above: The interior of the temple at Karnak showing the Great Hall in an early eighteenth-century print.

Opposite: The names of Set I, in hieroglyphs, decorate his tomb, so that in the afterlife there would be no doubt who he was or what he had achieved in life.

Above: The pillared hall inside the great temple at Abu Simbel, with figures that are 30 feet high.

Administration

The king or pharaoh had absolute authority and was regarded as a god himself, which put him on a level above all other humans. In life, he was thought of as a manifestation of the god Ra. In death, he became a form of Osiris. The king was a vital intermediary between gods and men. Through his daily rituals in the temple, he ensured that the gods looked kindly on humans.

In practice, of course, his authority also depended on his ability to administer the state, his success in controlling dissident elements, in defending Egypt from its enemies, and in waging successful campaigns that added to the wealth of the country. By the time of the New Kingdom, the pharaoh was expected to be a warrior king who led his people into battle.

The building of the pyramids and the great temples was a means of underlining his power. The elevation of certain gods or the adoption of certain cults throughout the country, coincided with the emergence of new dynasties who linked their fortunes with those of local gods taking on a national status. The process was reciprocal: Local gods grew in influence with the increase in power of local rulers. Marriages among the gods were as important as marriages between the rulers. Kings and gods from different areas made influential alliances that benefited the stability of the state and therefore the stability of the ordinary people as well.

Under the pharaoh, Egypt was divided into nomes or provinces. There came to be twenty-two nomes in Upper Egypt and twenty in Lower Egypt, each with its own capital and its own local god. The nomes were governed by nomarchs who were responsible for local taxation, justice, and an armed force. The stability of the country depended on the nomarchs being directly responsible to the king. Under a weak king, the nomarchs started to flex their muscles and give vent to their own ambitions; even initiating a new dynasty or enabling the intrusion of a foreign power.

The vizier or prime minister was the middle man between the king and the nomarchs; he was the most important person in the kingdom beneath the king. In effect, the vizier governed the land on behalf of the king, controlling almost every aspect of state administration, from territorial disputes and taxes to cattle census and rainfall measurement. He controlled agriculture and irrigation, was responsible for roads, buildings, the appointment of magistrates, and he dealt with foreign emissaries. The Egyptians had great respect for careful records of almost everything. The vizier's office kept records, for example, of royal decrees, of harvest and granaries, the census of the people, and private wills and contracts.

In the New Kingdom and possibly earlier, the role of vizier was duplicated with one vizier for Upper Egypt and one for Lower Egypt. Increasingly throughout Egyptian history, the government became more and more centralized as the king tried to keep a grip on his vast lands. Nubia eventually had its own viceroy directly responsible to the king. Viziers were usually related to the royal family although the most famous of them, Imhotep (of the third dynasty), was a commoner. Royal princes were often trained by being placed in the office of the vizier to learn about their future responsibilities.

Below: A painting from Abu Simbel depicting Ramesses II smiting an enemy with the god Horus on the right apparently encouraging him.

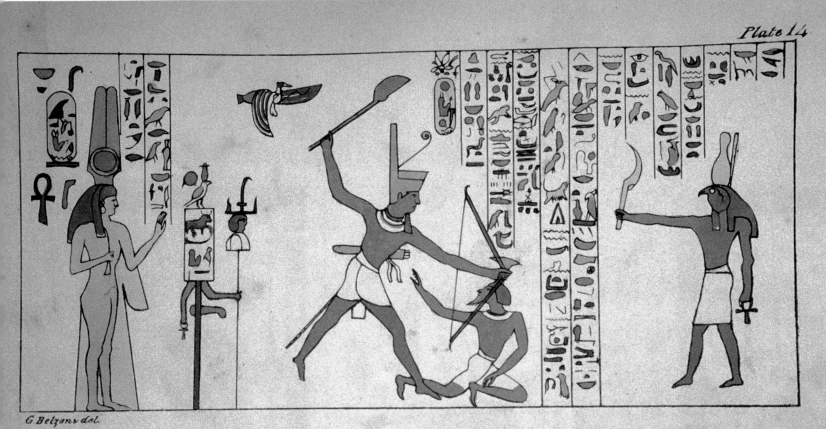

G. Belzoni del.

FROM THE GREAT TEMPLE OF JBSAMBUL IN NUBIA.

The Pharaoh: Ramesses II

The third king of the nineteenth dynasty was one of the best known and most successful of all the pharaohs who ruled Egypt. Known as Ramesses the Great, he was the son of Seti I and was already waging campaigns abroad with his father when he was only fourteen. He also began some of his great works of construction even before his father died. He succeeded to the throne when he was thirty and ruled for sixty-six years.

Ramesses waged campaigns against the Nubians, the Syrians, and the Hittites

whom he bested at the famous Battle of Kadesh which made him greatly renown at home and abroad. Despite being ambushed, he fought his way free and forced the Hittites to a peaceful settlement. He was also famous for the buildings he commissioned. The greatest ones were the temples at Abu Simbel and a temple to Ptah at Memphis. He added to the complex of temples at Karnak and built the famous Ramesseum, his mortuary temple at Thebes.

Although Ramesses had only four main wives, two of whom were his daughters, he is reputed to have had a total of 200 wives and concubines and more than 150 sons and daughters. We can tell from his mummified remains that he was exceptionally tall, with a sharply accentuated face, and close-set eyes. Like so many Egyptians, he evidently had bad teeth and arthritis. This was hardly surprising since he was ninety-six when he died. It was also clear that he had suffered from smallpox, and one other indignity: He had his genitals removed when he was mummified and they were placed in a special casket.

The Army

The Egyptians were not traditionally a warlike people. They preferred a peaceful existence, working the land and enjoying their pleasures. In times of invasion, they rose energetically to defend their country and this military zeal was harnessed by the king to expand the borders of Egypt and win new lands and greater wealth. But the enthusiasm of the average Egyptian for war waxed and waned, depending on the rewards. In many periods the king had to rely largely on mercenary troops, including Nubians and Libyans, who were the traditional enemies of Egypt. This, in turn, exposed Egypt to internal dangers.

Old Kingdom warriors had battle axes, lances, clubs and bows and arrows. Later, broad daggers, spears, and round-topped shields were introduced. Soldiers were called together for particular expeditions which might involve as much mining and construction as they did fighting. On one expedition we know that 3,000 soldiers received two jugs of water and twenty rolls of bread each per day.

After the war with the Hyksos, more powerful composite bows were introduced

Left: The three great pyramids at Giza, surrounded by lesser pyramids, truly remain one of the wonders of the world.

Above: Hieroglyphs at the Queen's Palace, Luxor. The discovery of the Rosetta Stone, with its parallel texts in different forms of language, first enabled scholars to interpret the ancient Egyptian hieroglyphs.

as well as scimitars and light chariots drawn by two horses, bearing an archer and driver. By the time of Ramesses II, soldiers wore tunics or an armor of leather and sometimes even crocodile skin.

Justice and the Law

Justice was an important concept to the Egyptians. Although no code of law has survived, records of certain cases and judgments have. There was a system of local courts and there were national courts for more severe crimes. People queued each day to have their case heard or to present their complaint to the judges. Priests and private individuals might sit as judges or magistrates for civil cases but the king or the vizier appointed special judges for important cases. There was great concern to give everyone an equal chance to have their case heard, regardless of their social status or wealth.

The Eloquent Peasant of Herakleopoli (who lived in the tenth dynasty) became immensely popular because he complained against the legal system of the time. He had suffered harsh treatment at the hands of local officials and eventually managed to get his complaint heard by the king. He repeatedly argued that "righteousness is for eternity" and this phrase eventually won him the king's ear and royal support. His popularity was based on his constant complaint against the judges that they should not give privilege to the wealthy but give the poor equal justice. His words were recorded and have survived in papyri. He symbolized the independence of the individual.

Priests and Temples

The priests who served the gods in their temples and who performed the rituals and festival ceremonies, played an enormously important part in Egyptian life. They dressed simply in white linen unless their rank allowed them to wear additional garments such as a leopard skin. They shaved their heads and were supposed to live pure lives, observe diets with certain taboos, and be totally loyal to their temple. They were allowed to marry and often passed down positions to their children.

There were various ranks of priests, ranging from those who kept the temples clean to those who officiated at the most important festivals. They alone had access to the innermost sanctuaries of the temple where they looked after its gods and goddesses, bringing them out occasionally for the public to admire. A modest temple might have twenty or thirty priests attached to it. A large temple might have hundreds or even thousands of priests, and huge wealth arising from land and possessions. Some priests even became ambitious and sought political advancement or greater wealth.

The great temple of Karnak at Thebes was dedicated to the god Amon and is one of the most extraordinary buildings anywhere in the world. Starting as a simple shrine in the time of the Middle Kingdom it grew, over a period of almost 2000 years, to cover 250 acres of temples, shrines, columns, statues, halls and court-yards. It had a sacred lake, massive gateways or pylons, colonnades, elaborate reliefs, obelisks and many other subsidiary constructions. The temple was linked to the Nile by a canal and by a row of sphinxes to the neighboring temple at Luxor, which was also dedicated to the god Amon.

Some of the greatest building took place between the eighteenth and twentieth dynasties under pharaohs such as Amenhotep III, Seti I, Ramesses II and III. The names of other famous pharaohs are linked to Karnak, such as Tuthmosis I and III and Queen Hatsheput. Even today, its massive columns and monumental scale are daunting. The temple as a whole represented an enormous commitment of faith and confidence by successive generations and an accumulation of religious weight to the prestige and dominance of the god and those pharaohs associated with him. Karnak was a political and social statement as much as a religious and ritual complex.

Pyramids and Burial

Egyptian life and ambition culminated in death. So many of the gods and goddesses were responsible either for helping Egyptians into the world or helping them out of it. Belief in the afterlife was immensely strong and the forms of burial hugely important. If temples symbolized the power and dignity of life, tombs were symbols of faith in death.

In the Old Kingdom, the royal and aristocratic tomb was the mastaba, a rectangular structure with a flat roof and an underground burial chamber. Over time, they became increasingly elaborate with false doors, hidden chambers, and inner

Above: The royal vulture, with its wings spread protectively outward, proudly decorates the tomb of Set I.

courtyards. The first pyramids were essentially a series of mastabas of ever decreasing size placed on top of each other. This was the construction of Imhotep's step pyramid at Saqqarah. It followed the form of a bent pyramid with smooth sides, but the angle turned inward half way up because the architects could not achieve the steepness of a real pyramid.

True pyramids, with straight sides coming to a point at the top, reached their best in the fourth dynasty with the famous pyramids at Giza, near modern Cairo. Khufu's pyramid was originally 754 feet (230 m) square at the base and more than 479 feet (146 m) high, surrounded by a complex of other buildings and courtyards. Limestone blocks were used to build the pyramid, with a casing of dressed limestone, and a granite burial chamber for the king inside the pyramid, which was 138 feet (42 m) above ground level. Construction of the pyramid may have taken up to twenty years and involved thousands of workers. When the king was placed inside, the burial chamber and access tunnels were blocked and the entrance sealed. Even so, the chambers were looted but this does not seem to have dented the Egyptian faith in everlasting life.

Later kings built other elaborate tombs and mortuary complexes. In the eighteenth and nineteenth dynasties, they dug tombs deep in the rock in what is known as the Valley of the Kings (there was also a Valley of the Queens) on the western bank of the Nile opposite Thebes. The tombs were reached by long tunnels which were set up with traps to foil robbers, but these deterrents rarely worked and many of the tombs were robbed quite shortly after the burial of the pharaoh. One of the few that survived was the famous tomb of the young Tutankhamun. The magnificent artifacts that it contained revealed for modern eyes not only the immense material wealth and superb craftsmanship of ancient Egypt but also an absolute confidence that life in this world would continue even more splendidly in another. Such confidence should win our respect.

Index

Picture Credits